MACBETH

Teacher's Guide

Copyright © 1989 Harcourt Brace Jovanovich Canada Inc.
55 Horner Avenue, Toronto, Ontario
M8Z 4X6

Canadian Cataloguing in Publication Data

Roy, Ken
  Macbeth. Teacher's guide

(HBJ Shakespeare)
Includes text of the play.
Supplement to: Shakespeare, William, 1564–1616.
Macbeth.
Bibliography: p. 30, 45–46
ISBN 0-7747-1291-0

1. Shakespeare, William, 1564–1616. Macbeth.
I. Law, Harriet, 1931–   . II. Kortes, Margaret.
III. Shakespeare, William, 1564–1616. Macbeth.
IV. Title.   V. Series.

PR2823.R69   1988   822.3′3   C89-093056-2

Printed in Canada

88 89 90 91 92   5 4 3 2 1

HBJ SHAKESPEARE

MACBETH

Teacher's Guide

Series Editor: Ken Roy
Contributing Author: Harriet Law
Notes for Macbeth: Margaret Kortes

Harcourt Brace Jovanovich, Canada

Toronto   Orlando   San Diego   London   Sydney

Table of Contents

Shakespeare's England

Approaches to *HBJ Shakespeare's Macbeth*

An Introduction to *HBJ Shakespeare*

PHILOSOPHY OF *HBJ SHAKESPEARE*

HBJ Shakespeare was developed in response to a growing need for an integrated language arts and student-centred approach to the study of Shakespeare. By providing a wide range of writing, speaking/listening, viewing, and independent project activities that allow for personal and creative response, this series assists students to recognize both the accessibility of Shakespeare's plays and the relevancy of the plays to their own experience, and gives them the opportunity to further explore Shakespeare in ways meaningful to them.

Students are encouraged to become familiar with and involved in the plays from the beginning of their reading by using these features common to all *HBJ Shakespeare* editions.

TEXT FEATURES

- Getting started – provides students with activities related to important themes in the play for discussion and/or written response.

- In this scene – gives students a brief scene description, allowing them to anticipate the issues they will encounter in the scene.

- For the next scene – offers students one or two predictive questions that draw upon their experience and provides them with a bridge to the next scene.

- Text notes – provide students with explanations for Shakespeare's text and help eliminate difficulties students may have with the language. These notes appear on pages that are facing the Shakespeare text and are aligned with the line(s) of text they explain.

- Illustrations – contribute detailed and historically accurate visual representations of characters and events. Illustrations appear at the beginning of each act and at the beginning of most scenes and help the students enter the world of the play.

- Activities – provide for personal writing, speaking, reading, viewing, and independent project responses from students at the end of scenes, following each act, and at the end of the play.

THE ACTIVITIES

The activities encourage students to explore further the issues they considered before and during their reading of the scenes. These interpretive and creative activities appear after all major scenes, after groupings of minor scenes, and at the end of acts. Activities that consider the whole text appear at the end of the play. Many of the activities are recommended for group work. (All the benefits of group work — such as accepting responsibility for learning, using expressive and receptive modes of communication in brainstorming, problem solving, and establishing a shared goal — can be derived as well from the study of Shakespeare as they can from any other areas of study.) In selecting and completing individual activities, students discover opportunities to:

- discuss the play, drawing upon their own experience;
- discuss and/or write about their feelings and responses to characters, situations, and concepts;
- make generalizations they can apply to new situations;
- complete independent learning projects;
- keep personal journals;
- create directors' logs;
- improvise, role play, or dramatize scene segments;
- make video recordings.

The activities at the end of acts and at the end of the play are generally intended to synthesize students' experiences of the scenes within the act. Many of these activities will require more time to complete than the end-of-scene activities.

Note: It is not expected that students should complete all activities at the end of a scene or complete activities for all scenes. Students and/or teachers should select activities appropriate to the students' interests and abilities.

HBJ Shakespeare allows students to join in the learning process by becoming actively involved in the play. We hope teachers and students will share in this dynamic experience of Shakespeare with both a feeling of comfort and a sense of confidence.

AN OVERVIEW OF THE TEACHER GUIDE

Section II of this guide offers strategies for presenting *HBJ Shakespeare* and for presenting a play in a condensed time period (approximately three to five weeks).

Section III offers historical and interpretive information about Shakespeare's England.

Section IV includes

- a brief historical background to *Macbeth*,
- a note on historical revisionism and Shakespeare's sources for *Macbeth*,
- a note on contemporary background,
- a note on the stage history of *Macbeth*,
- strategies for presenting *Macbeth* in a condensed time period,
- a selection of classroom resources, and a list of references cited.

Suggested Strategies for Presenting *HBJ Shakespeare*

INTRODUCING AN HBJ SHAKESPEARE PLAY

If this is your students' first experience with Shakespeare, or their first experience with *HBJ Shakespeare*, you might wish to assist them in becoming comfortable with the text by allowing them time to discover and discuss the following features:

- the letter To the Reader that introduces students to the response-based approach they will find through the book and the Getting Started section that has them begin to consider important themes by drawing upon their own experience;

- the layout of Shakespeare text on right-hand pages and text explanatory notes on left-hand pages. Text notes are aligned as much as possible with the text they explain;

- Dramatis Personae – the list of characters in the play;

- visuals which appear at the beginning of each act and before most scenes;

- the "In this scene . . ." paragraphs which appear at the beginning of each act and scene and focus on important issues in the scene;

- the "For the next scene . . ." questions which appear on the page preceding each new scene and act so that students will draw upon their own experiences as they make the transition from one scene to another;

- activities which appear at the beginning of the play, at the end of most scenes, and at the end of the play. These activities have students explore many levels of thinking as they apply inferential, analytical, interpretive, and creative responses to the tasks they choose to complete individually and/or in group situations. The activities provide students with personal response-based opportunities to direct their own learning as they experience the play.

EXPERIENCING THE PLAY

You and your students might wish to discuss and record reasons for studying the play. After students have discussed and/or written their responses to the letter To the Reader and Getting Started questions, introduce the first two scenes by having students read "In this scene . . ." for both. Students could then read, view, or listen to the scenes to get an overall impression of the plot and character development. Clarify any language or vocabulary difficulties students may have. Give students time to record individual responses to scenes and acts in their journals. Provide time for them to discover, react to, and record their individual responses to scenes and acts using the activities.

USING THE ACTIVITIES

The activities following scenes and acts have students use inferential, analytical, interpretive, and creative skills in their responses. Students should always be clear about the teacher's expectations for completing these tasks meaningfully. Note that because activities vary in scope and require varying lengths of time to complete, students will need assistance in selecting activities, and time provided for them to share or present their responses.

No one grouping of activities in an *HBJ Shakespeare* play will fit all class situations. It is extremely important, therefore, for the teacher to plan ahead, know the abilities and interests of the class, and have clearly stated objectives for the presentation of the scenes, acts, and activities to be undertaken.

Because many of the activities at the end of acts require more than the assignment portion of class time to complete, students should have the opportunity to work on them as the class study of the scenes progresses.

Care should be taken not to overload students with activity tasks. It is important to remember that although some students have developed skills in directing their own learning and are able to select and complete activities, others will need practice and support in developing these skills.

An overview of activities found in *HBJ Shakespeare* and strategies for facilitating student response to them follows.

Writing Activities
The writing activities present opportunities for students to write in a variety of modes and genres, for different purposes, and to different

audiences. These activities include writing items such as news articles, press releases, psychological reports, interviews, letters, journals, and editorials. To integrate a full writing program (including pre-writing, revising, and publishing activities) with the study of Shakespeare in a limited amount of time, you might choose a sequence of procedures such as the following:

Pre-writing
Pre-writing is often an on-going activity in which the student rehearses ideas for possible inclusion in writing assignments. The product of pre-writing could be a journal entry or notes made to prepare for a particular type of writing.

Students reading *Hamlet* might, for example, write a news report issued by the Palace Corps about Claudius's decision to send Hamlet to England. As a pre-writing activity they may wish to make notes about structures and styles of news reporting they observed when comparing the same news event written in several different newspapers.

Revising
Revising can occur at any time during the writing process. If students wish to have peer feedback before revising writing assignments, they could arrange peer group conferences. As a student reads his/her writing in progress, and points out a difficulty, other members of the group could offer ideas that may have worked for them in resolving a similar problem.

Publishing
Before students publish their written material, they may wish to apply a checklist including items such as points of grammar, punctuation, and syntax to their work. Students could publish a casebook or newspaper about the play, containing their writings during/at the end of the study of the play. They may prefer to put their news reports on the bulletin board following the revision stage.

Journal Activities
Students may wish to keep journals – a personal record of responses to issues in the text. Sometimes, these entries will be private reflections. Many entries, however, will be ones that students would enjoy sharing with a peer, in a group, with the teacher, or with the whole class. Teachers lend authenticity and demonstrate a commitment to writing by using the class writing time to create their own journal writing entries as writing models. These entries should also be shared.

The following is an extension of a journal activity. It is from the Act 1 "Consider the Whole Act" Activities for *Julius Caesar*.

Read through all of the journal entries you have made so far. Draw up a summary entry for Act 1. Use the following questions to help you:

- What have I discovered about the life and conditions of Rome in 44 B.C.?

- What have I learned about _____ ? (Fill in the name of several major characters.)

- What are some particularly interesting things about Scene 1, Scene 2, and Scene 3 in terms of the way they are presented to the audience?

Independent Learning Project Activities

Independent learning project activities provide students with the opportunity to direct their own learning as they explore new areas of study or develop skills to complete tasks they set for themselves. Many students show considerable aptitude for completing independent research and learning assignments while others may need practice and support in developing the necessary skills for acquiring knowledge independently. The independent learning project activities in *HBJ Shakespeare* are recognizable by their recommendations that students: 1) discuss the activity with the teacher and 2) keep their notes and rough drafts for the activity in a separate folder.

The following is an example of an independent activity. It is from the Act 1, Scene 1 Activities for *Romeo and Juliet*.

There are references to the mythological god and goddess Cupid and Diana in this scene. Find out as much as you can about each of these characters. What significance do they have for Romeo in this scene? Why have mythological characters such as Cupid and Diana remained so popular to readers, viewers, and writers, to the present day?

As you do research, discuss your work with the teacher to make sure you are on the right track. Keep all your notes and rough drafts in a folder.

Present a summary of your findings in an essay, a chart, or an audio-visual form at the end of the time specified for this independent activity.

The completed assignments may be presented to the teacher/class independently or in a group presentation such as a debate, a seminar, or a video presentation.

Scene Rehearsal Activities

These activities allow students to develop their dramatic perceptions of the play as they consider motivations for speeches and ways of choreographing actions, and requirements for settings and props.

When students consider the physical dimensions of an action, they often find that the dramatic content becomes clearer in their minds. For example, students often have difficulty following the sequential movement and seating arrangements in the banquet scene in *Macbeth*; but when they choreograph the scene, they gain a clearer sense of what happens and are better able to understand the cause of Macbeth's hallucinations. Likewise, when students act out the confused activity of the characters around the bushes in Act 3, Scene 1, of *A Midsummer Night's Dream*, they better understand the significance of the Duke's speech about imagination in Act 5, Scene 1.

Students could rehearse scene segments in small groups. While students are acting, you could move from group to group observing and highlighting problems they are experiencing rather than offering solutions. When students raise questions about their problems in interpreting lines dramatically, you could ask, "Why is that a problem for you?" You might ask questions such as "Would the character be standing or sitting when he/she says the lines?" "Why do you think so?" Then look for a group that has prepared an interesting interpretation of a scene segment and have them present it to the class.

Director's Log Activities

A director's log is a recording, either in note form or tape, of the ideas the group's scene-rehearsal leader wishes to keep for reference.

After a group rehearsing a scene segment chooses its director, he/she becomes responsible for conducting the group through problems it may have interpreting scene speeches and actions.

The director's log is the official record of decisions the group has reached with regard to the interpretations and the staging of the scene segment. It might include information such as

- how the group will create the scene segment,
- how the group will choreograph the action,
- where the group will place the action,
- what predominant mood the group will create for the action.

The log might also include the group's differences of opinion related to speeches, actions, and staging.

The log could record, as well, events that precede and follow the scene segment to give it context.

Directors who tape discussion related to scene-segment interpretations often find that their group gains helpful insights to the dynamics of idea-sharing by listening to the taped discussions.

The director's log activity is a useful strategy for having students combine some or all of the following skills: speaking, listening, writing, and problem-solving.

Improvisation Activities

Students often like to speculate about different characters' behaviour. By improvising, students often understand the behaviour of these characters better. It is easier for students to improvise a scene segment than it is for them to write a summary of the scene. When students improvise, they gain a sense of the character's motivation. Directors often use improvisation as a way of warming up actors for their roles. In improvisation activities, students use their imagination and their personal experiences to transform characters' speeches and so enlarge the life of the characters in their minds.

Listening Activities

Recordings
Recordings of selected scenes or specific speeches can be used to spark discussion about characters' motives and feelings.

Music
Students might enjoy choosing and taping music they feel would appropriately accompany a particular scene. A student (or group) preparing a reading of the scene could choose the music; or you could have one student (or group) prepare a reading while another prepares the "theme" music.

Viewing Activities

Film
To provide students with a sense of the whole play, you might set aside two or three periods for this viewing activity. Watching a film of the play before class study allows students to:

- acquire a sense of the plot, character relations, and shape of the play in one experience;
- appreciate the historical aspect of the play by seeing the costumes;

- gain a sense of the setting;
- become familiar with the language; and
- see the integration of language with character and actions.

Make a Video

This activity is time-consuming and requires careful planning and close monitoring. The time needed, from script to show-time, is approximately three weeks. Even the camera-shy student can become involved in the activity in some capacity. This activity stresses process as much as product and while it is a video activity, it is also a writing-process activity: it teaches concepts about narrative construction, characterization, setting, theme, and symbols, point of view; and the importance of proofreading, editing, and revising. Perhaps most important, it teaches co-operation and team work.

Although students are eager to grab a camera and begin shooting at the mere mention of the word "video," the camera shoot should always be preceded by a written or sketched series of visuals, or a "shot" list.

WHAT TO SHOOT

Establish time limits. Teachers and students should be aware that it can take from three to five classroom hours to shoot about ten minutes of finished video material. It is very important to select segments from the text that are not too long or complicated, that don't involve too many characters, that are neither too static nor too frenetic, and that are not dialogue-dominated. Have students shoot a sequence that does not go beyond fifteen minutes finished viewing time because it is simply too difficult to sustain evenness of quality in a longer shoot. Once students have decided on three or four possible scene segments, through rehearsed readings, have them test the segments.

CREATE A SHOOTING SCRIPT

This activity is the most important. It requires students to break down the text into "shooting pieces" in which the audio and the visual must support each other. The visual must highlight and support the audio (text, music, sound effects). To prepare for this part of the activity, students could divide a page in half and label one side audio and the other side video. This page will act as their storyboard. Note: a bad storyboard is a bad video.

When they edit their shooting script, have students consider the following:

A. *Video*

- Is each shot completely described? Do the visuals follow logically?
- Do the visuals maintain unity of impression? Is there an indication of what shot to use?
- Is the angle of the shots clearly indicated and is the mood consistent?
- Is the lighting effective and logical?
- Are the directions to the camera director included for each shot?
- Are the shots requiring action carefully blocked and well-rehearsed?

B. *Audio*

- Does the audio script support and reinforce the video portion? Will the audio fit the time allowed in the visual shot?
- Is the dialogue clear and logical? Is the audio script clear and coherent?
- Does the audio script support and balance the visual script?
- Is the audio script free from embarrassing mechanical errors?

THE FINISHED PRODUCT

- Have the videos transferred to one tape for a class video day. The class could be arranged as if students were viewing an important film screening; members of the audience could prepare and present reviews.
- The videos could be presented to a school assembly.
- The videos could provide the basis for a workshop given by the producers to students from another class who would like to undertake a similar project.
- Students might give a brief oral presentation about the importance of the writing process to the visual media.
- Finally, students could write papers on the process and difficulties of scripting a scene segment for video.

Video activities can be either group or entire class endeavours, depending on the class size. All class members can be involved with some aspect of the project. The following are some suggestions:

- technical personnel – camera operators, sound consultants, set-up staff, director, lighting consultant, set designer, prop designer, music co-ordinators

- on-camera personnel – actors, narrators, commentators
- advertising personnel – poster designers, radio ad creators, publicity personnel

EVALUATION OF THE ACTIVITIES

Evaluation is an integral part of the teaching/learning process. Handled wisely and sensitively, it can enhance the learning process provided that *objectives are clear, those objectives are communicated to the students,* and *those objectives form the basis of the evaluation process.* If careful attention is given to developing effective techniques for evaluating the process and product of students' activity-based learning, the evaluation will foster student-teacher trust, aid in measuring student progress accurately, and facilitate the entire learning process.

In *HBJ Shakespeare*, students are asked to complete activities which require the use of a wide range of skills in areas such as listening, speaking, reading, writing, viewing, problem-solving, and performing. They are asked to participate in activities by using group interaction skills and independent learning skills.

In evaluating student performance, teachers could consider these criteria:

- student understanding of the task;
- student attitude toward the task;
- variety of approaches used by the student;
- acceptance of responsibility for the task.

In group activity evaluation, teachers could consider the following:

- student willingness to accept suggestions from others;
- student attitude in discussion groups;
  - how well the student encouraged others in the group;
  - how well the student responded to suggestions from the group;
  - how well the student shared leadership and responsibility with other members of the group.

This information will help the teacher to assist the students in developing sound work habits, study and research skills, and social-interaction skills.

Throughout the *HBJ Shakespeare* activities are recommendations for students to employ *peer evaluation* as well as *self-evaluation* strategies in their approach to their learning experience.

The following are some ideas to consider in evaluating the process and product of students' work.

Writing Activities

These activities, which likely form the bulk of the student product, can be evaluated in ways such as the following:

- by formal writing assignments in which checklists are presented as the evaluation criteria;
- by journal or private writing activities;
- by a variety of writing folder activities.

Writing is usually evaluated using broad headings such as content, organization, ideas, mechanics, style, diction, use of language conventions, and originality.

Speaking activities

Evaluation of speaking skills is best accomplished in small group learning situations, dramatic enactments, role-playing activities, group and/or partner discussions, debates, interviews, panel discussions, and choral reading tasks. Speaking skills could be evaluated using criteria such as, does the student contribute ideas freely? make responses respectfully? take turns willingly?

Listening activities

Evaluation of listening skills is best accomplished during a group activity. That way student performance can be assessed in a give-and-take situation involving peers in a dynamic shared-leadership, problem-solving activity. Listening activities can be evaluated best by teacher observation of group participation in problem-solving activities.

The following checklist could be applied to the listening process:

- does the student listen quietly and attentively?
- does the student offer comments such as, "I see what you mean"; "The way I see it is . . . "; "I think this will work because . . . "; "I don't think this will work because . . . "

Problem-solving activities

Problem solving underlies all learning and happens most effectively when teachers and students are equal partners in the process. In *HBJ Shakespeare*, teachers have many opportunities to observe students' problem-solving skills as they participate in role-playing, scene-rehearsing, and other drama activities, and as they complete independent learning projects and viewing activities.

The following checklist could be applied to the problem-solving process:

- does the student hypothesize, synthesize, make analogies, and recognize possibilities?
- when considering unfamiliar concepts, does the student refer to personal experience as a basis for exploring varieties of materials in order to move from the known to unknown?
- does the student discuss, read, make educated guesses, and predictions about abstract concepts?

Independent learning project activities
In keeping with the purpose and approach of this series, the independent learning projects should be evaluated both for *process* and *product*.

In evaluating any of the *HBJ Shakespeare* activities, it is important for teachers to remember that the purposes of the activities are both to allow students to become a dynamic part of their learning experience and to encourage them to reach beyond their present abilities and extend themselves further than a teacher might take them in a teacher-centred environment.

Presenting *HBJ Shakespeare* in a Condensed Time Period

Some teachers may need to present the Shakespeare play in a condensed time period (approximately three to five weeks). The following suggestions offer ways to present the play using the student-centred approach in this series.

SINGLE FOCUS APPROACH

The class could preview part or all of the play by viewing a film to establish a focus for experiencing the play, such as one of the following:

- a main theme,
- a main character,
- the plot-line itself.

Having chosen one of the above as their primary focus in reading the text, students could then select to complete the activities related to that focus.

Single character focus

Shakespeare characters who are vital and inherent parts of the play experience and whose behaviour profoundly affects the plot development are appropriate choices for understanding and responding to the whole play through the single character focus.

In *Julius Caesar*, for example, it is Brutus (whom we first encounter in Act 1, Scene 2), whose behaviour most significantly brings the plot to its climax and denouement. The main themes of the play are revealed in his decisions and actions. Through Brutus, the personal and political conflicts of the play are resolved. Brutus, then, is a vital character in this play.

After choosing Brutus as their single character focus for *Julius Caesar*, students could direct their attention to parts of important scenes that include Brutus. Scenes such as the ones in the first two acts that introduce students to Brutus's strengths and weaknesses, and to the important decisions he makes; to the assassination scene;

the funeral scene; the final farewell between Brutus and Cassius; and Brutus's death might be considered. Students could then complete activities which focus on Brutus to further explore the language of the play, the relationships between Brutus and others, and his character.

In using the single character focus, students have an opportunity to observe and respond to the play in depth within the condensed time allotment.

STORY-TELLING AND/OR VIDEO APPROACH

A detailed study of each scene is not necessary for providing a complete learning experience of the play. It is quite possible for students to experience parts of a play without reading the script itself. Students often respond enthusiastically to the integrity and vibrancy of the dramatic experience when the play is brought to life by a story-telling or video presentation.

Similarly, students can fully appreciate the drama of the play when they see it on video. Students who are encouraged to respond critically to the choices made by actors, directors, and designers as they watch Shakespeare being performed, are likely to become enthusiastic and discriminating theatre-goers and media-viewers.

KEY SCENES APPROACH

After you and your students have previewed the play to decide what aspect (characters, theme, plot-line) is of most interest, you might designate segments of the play for attention. Below is a suggested procedure for approaching the five acts in a condensed time period.

One-third of the time for Act 1
Act 1 should be given careful attention so that characters and their motivations are clearly established, the issues and themes are made clear, and the plot is clarified. You may prefer to do this by playing a recording, by showing a video or movie version of the act, by using rehearsed readings, or by group discussions. Whatever method you choose, it should be one with which the students feel comfortable.

A focussed study of the first act of the play is important. It gives students the opportunity to identify characters and their motives, themes, and essential conflicts. Once they have familiarized themselves with the first act, students will feel more comfortable completing the activities throughout the rest of the play.

At the end of students' experience with Act 1, they may find that by completing activities from "Consider the Whole Act" they gain clearer impressions and understandings of the act's key issues.

One-third of the time for Acts 2 and 3
Select important plot development and/or character interaction scenes to use as springboards for class discussion and involvement in end-of-act/scene activities related to key issues. Since it is impossible to have students explore all the play's conflicts and themes, assist students in determining topics they may choose to develop in their activity response.

Students could make journal entry responses to scenes from Acts 2 and 3 that are not focussed during class time.

One-third of the time for Acts 4 and 5
Focus on key scenes from Acts 4 and 5. The last scene of Act 5 should include discussion about the major conflicts, issues, and themes in the play, recalling discussions about them in Act 1, so that students experience a sense of completion.

A final writing, dramatic, or viewing activity could result from this discussion. The group might wish to have a "video day" viewing of the ending of a film or video version of the play. They could choose to have a discussion about the play as tragedy (comedy, history) or to present a dramatization of selected segments of student-prepared scenes. Students might wish to debate major issues in the play.

Summing up is important because it leaves the play complete in students' minds and, although not all the issues will have been covered, students will have achieved their own experience of Shakespeare.

See Suggested Strategies for Teaching *Macbeth* in a Condensed Time Period, page T40.

Shakespeare's England

HBJ Shakespeare encourages students to bring their experiences to the play. Like Shakespeare's audiences, students know about love, loyalty, taboos, leadership, revenge, identity, and ambition. As Shakespeare wrote in a time very distant from and different to our own, however, students will likely better appreciate the plays if they have some context for Shakespeare's world. You might wish to use the historical information that follows as your own resource and discuss these topics with students during their study of the play. A bibliography for Shakespeare's England appears on page **T30**.

WHO WAS WILLIAM SHAKESPEARE?

During Shakespeare's lifetime (1564–1616), England was ruled by Elizabeth I (1558–1603) and James I (1603–1625). Because Shakespeare was a commoner and only the nobility kept formal chronicles of themselves, we have only a few facts about his life. He was baptized on April 26, 1564, at Stratford-upon-Avon. Since it was customary to baptize on the third day, we can assume he was born on April 23. We know that he was the third of John Shakespeare's and Mary Arden's eight children and that his father was a glove-maker, a grain-dealer, and a man of some importance in the town who served as alderman and mayor.

Shakespeare attended a grammar school in Stratford-upon-Avon where the chief emphasis (as in all such schools) was on Latin. How long he remained there is not certain, but in 1583, at the age of eighteen, he married Anne Hathaway. Her home, in the adjacent village of Shottery, is now known as Anne Hathaway's cottage and has long been a main tourist attraction for Stratford visitors. The couple had three children: Susannah, born in 1583, and twins, Hamnet and Judith, born in 1585. Susannah married and had a child, Elizabeth, who also married, but she had no children. Hamnet died in 1596, at the age of eleven. Judith married, but her children did not live. In three short generations, the direct lineage of Shakespeare died out.

Sometime between 1585 and 1591, Shakespeare moved to London where we assume he spent most of his adult life. How he became an actor and a playwright we don't know, but we do know that he became one of the chief stockholders in the most important theatre company of the time (the Lord Chamberlain's Men) and a part owner of the Globe theatre. We also know that he became famous enough to draw a scathing insult from another playwright, an envious one perhaps, named Robert Greene, who called him "an upstart crow, beautified with our feathers."

When the Lord Chamberlain's Men were taken under the patronage of King James I, their name was changed to the King's Men. In this company were some of London's best actors, including Richard Burbage and Will Kempe. Shakespeare both wrote and acted for this company.

In London, Shakespeare made enough money to buy a coat of arms, giving himself the official status of "gentleman." For unknown reasons, he returned to Stratford-upon-Avon in 1612 to live in one of its finest houses, New Place. He lived there until he died, at age fifty-two, on the date of his birth.

The exact dates for Shakespeare's plays are not known. The following list gives a general frame of reference:

COMEDIES	TRAGEDIES	HISTORIES
1591		Henry VI, Part I
1592 The Comedy of Errors		Henry VI, Part II
1592 Two Gentlemen of Verona		Henry VI, Part III
1593 Love's Labour's Lost	Titus Andronicus	Richard III
1594		King John
1595 A Midsummer Night's Dream	Romeo and Juliet	Richard II
1596 The Merchant of Venice		
1596 Taming of the Shrew		
1597		Henry IV, Part I
1598 Much Ado About Nothing		Henry IV, Part II
1599 As You Like It	Julius Caesar	
1599 The Merry Wives of Windsor		Henry V
1601 Twelfth Night	Hamlet	
1602 Troilus and Cressida		
1602 All's Well That Ends Well		
1604 Measure for Measure	Othello	
1605	King Lear	
1606	Macbeth	
1607	Timon of Athens	
1607	Antony and Cleopatra	
1608 Pericles		
1609	Coriolanus	
1610 Cymbeline		
1611 The Winter's Tale		
1611 The Tempest		
1613		Henry VIII

WHAT WAS LONDON LIKE IN SHAKESPEARE'S TIME?

London in the 1590s was a bustling city of about 200,000 people. One of the first things that Shakespeare might have noticed was the great number of churches in the city. London was known as the city of churches.

The city was still walled as it had been for many years, but it was growing rapidly. People flocked to the city, causing a building boom of staggering proportions. The streets were narrow, cobble-stoned in places, but always dirty and crowded. Sanitation was unknown and plagues were common.

Shakespeare lived first in St. Helen's parish near Bishopgate Street and later near Cripplegate and across the river in Southwark. It was an exciting city for a young man from the country – full of strange sights and sounds. Since it was the age of exploration, there were many exotic sights such as clothing from the Arab countries, masks and charms from Africa, goods from China, and strange fruits and vegetables such as the tomato and the potato.

Since London was a port city, many languages were heard in the streets, such as French, Italian, Dutch, and Russian. A popular pas-time was learning to speak these new languages, particularly French. Londoners received their education by reading books which spread in profusion with the advent of the printing press. It is estimated that there were over fifty printing presses in operation in London during this time. There were no public libraries or newspapers but "broad-sides" (one page sheets printed on both sides) that reported news happenings in the community – especially murders, fires, deaths of important people, disasters of all kinds and, occasionally, bits of history – were sold for half a penny all over London on almost all street corners.

The streets were crammed with humanity. People begged for food and cried out for alms, shopkeepers called out to passersby to purchase their wares, balladeers sang on street corners, church bells called citizens to prayer, coaches clacked over the cobble-stones, and water-bearers staggered under their loads. Londoners worked a twelve-hour day.

In addition to the noisy, sprawling markets, there were shops everywhere imaginable. Clothing was sold on London Bridge. Gold-smiths, grocers, fishmongers, and ironmongers also staked out areas to sell their wares. Even the wall around London itself gave way to shops.

Londoners loved entertainment and much of it was free. There were water games on the Thames, a small zoo in the Tower of London, cock-fights, bear-baitings, public executions, and, of course, plays, including those of Shakespeare himself, that covered just about any subject a Londoner might be interested in.

Despite the roughness of the period, it was not necessarily an unkind environment. Londoners gave generously to the poor, and London merchants experimented with various methods of finding work for the poor and the unemployed. And there was Queen Elizabeth, who made frequent appearances to the delight of the citizens.

Permanent theatres were rapidly replacing the old inn-yards as places of entertainment, and great actors were emerging to form acting troupes. New playwrights were springing up to supply the theatres with new plays. Shakespeare arrived in London when the theatres were thriving. It was a wonderful and glorious time in which to be alive and working in one of the most vibrant cities in the world.

WHAT WERE THE THEATRES FOR SHAKESPEARE'S PLAYS LIKE?

Inn-yards were favourite places for play performances in Elizabethan England because they provided a ready-made audience and because their long, narrow entrances and surrounding balconies served as makeshift theatres.

Stages were probably improvised from any available materials – some must have been quite precarious. The inn's stables and out-buildings likely would have served as change rooms, and stage properties would have been at a minimum. In the early years of these productions, performers took up a collection at the end of each play. In later years, the performers contracted with the yard-keeper to have him charge admission.

As plays grew in popularity, some actors considered having a permanent facility for their work. James Burbage, a popular actor admired by Shakespeare, built one of the first permanent theatres in 1576. To pacify the Puritans, who believed that plays were sinful, Burbage built his playhouse, called the Theatre, outside the city walls in Shoreditch. In 1577, another theatre, the Curtain, was also built in Shoreditch. The problem with Shoreditch, however, was that patrons had to walk over fields and swamps to get there. For this reason, theatre builders later chose Bankside, an area across the river from the still theatre-prohibiting city, in what is now called Southwark. In 1587 the Rose was built in Southwark, and in 1595, the Swan was erected there.

When Richard, son of James Burbage, ran into difficulties with his landlord over renewing the lease for the land on which his father's playhouse stood, he decided to move. He entered into an agreement with five of his fellow actors, one of them being Shakespeare, to build a new theatre called the Globe on Bankside in 1599. The Globe had an octagonal shape with a "thrust" stage projecting into the body of the theatre so that an audience surrounded the actors on three sides. There were three levels of balconies which enclosed the stage and an open pit in the middle that accommodated the poorer patrons. Drawings of the Globe indicate that only the balconies and some of the pit and stage were covered by a thatch roof. The rest of the theatre was exposed to the elements.

The Globe's stage was primitive by our standards. It had doors on both sides for entrances and exits and a recessed area which could serve as an inner stage. There was little room for storage or props and elaborate scenery. Above the stage recess was a balcony, and the floor had a trap door. The stage could be used, therefore, to represent heaven, earth, and hell − symbolism that would have been readily understood by an Elizabethan audience.

The Elizabethan stage provided an intimacy between actor and audience not possible in modern curtained theatres. This intimacy was sometimes hazardous for the actor if the audience were unhappy with the performance. (Some audiences, disappointed with the performances, became quite violent.) Theatrical innovations, such as the soliloquy and other devices to indicate the speedy passage of time typical of Elizabethan theatre, worked well on this simple stage.

The last big Elizabethan theatre, built in 1600, and called the Fortune, was square, unlike the O-shaped theatres that had been the norm. A stage similar to the Fortune's square stage was built in Stratford, Ontario, in the Festival Theatre, during the 1960s. Today we can see plays written by Shakespeare presented in much the same way as they had been presented for the audiences of his time.

As quickly as they sprang up, the Elizabethan theatres with their thrust stages died out, in part because they were licensed to make money for the owners, who traded on a popular interest of the time, much as rock concert promoters do today. Elizabethan theatres fulfilled a need, and when that need died, so did the theatres.

The Actors
Since all Elizabethan actors were male, all female roles were played by boys or men. It was not easy for the actors to appear convincing in female roles in broad daylight to their highly critical Elizabethan audiences. Actors were also required to perform very stylized and difficult dances that often needed both superior acrobatic skills and exceptional physical stamina. The dancing requirements were likely easy in comparison to the fight scene requirements, however. Actors

were expected to fight as expert swordsmen. They needed technical skills and training as well as excellent physical conditioning to re-create duels and/or battle scenes without injuring themselves or their opponents. They had to perform actions such as running a sword through another actor's head or tearing out his entrails without impairing the opponent's usefulness for the next day's performance. Audiences of the day expected to see bloody deaths and mutilations in fight scenes. When bloodshed was involved, actors used sheep's blood because it had the right consistency for "running" well and it provided the audience with "real" blood. In stabbing scenes, actors wore concealed bladders of blood under their costumes. These bladders could be ruptured by retractable knife blades. When this action was performed correctly, the bladder worn by the character being stabbed was punctured, the blood spewed forth in profusion, and the audience cheered with glee. Performed badly, the actor being stabbed was injured (not an infrequent occurrence) and had to be carted off the stage, probably also to cheers from the audience. In this case another actor had to fill in. Since acting companies were small (perhaps twelve or fifteen men), actors were required to play many parts convincingly, often on short notice, and always to a demanding audience. Acting was a hazardous occupation in Elizabethan England!

The Audience

They were a rough group of people, usually consisting of working-men, trade apprentices from London, seamen on leave, and country visitors to the city in search of cheap entertainment. They were frequently noisy, boisterous, and given to violent outbursts of disapproval if their expectations were not met. They loved the sound effects, including cannons, drums, and chilling screams; the extravagant costumes; and the props, such as guillotines, fountains, and ladders. Most of these people stood on the ground, and so acquired their name, "groundlings." Dramatists like Shakespeare disliked these lower-class individuals and often portrayed them as humorously foolish and unsuccessful imitators of the educated people in their plays.

Surrounding the theatre were vendors, prostitutes, con-men, and pickpockets. Some patrons with money sat on benches in the balconies, while those who wanted to display their finery could rent stools on the stage. Members of the nobility may have attended the theatre for sheer adventure, but they usually arranged to have plays performed in their own homes.

The growing middle class attended a different type of theatre, which was indoors, had artificial lighting, special effects, a sophisticated satirical style, well-trained boy actors, and a higher entrance fee. Shakespeare's company of actors eventually purchased one of these "private" theatres (The Blackfriars), and produced many of his later plays there.

In an age in which the printing press widened literacy but could not possibly affect the lifestyle of the many illiterates, the theatre offered both a ready source of information and good entertainment.

WHAT WAS IT LIKE TO LIVE IN SHAKESPEARE'S TIME?

Shakespeare grew up in a chaotic period of history called the Renaissance. It was marked by both the vigour of powerful changes and the aftermath of drastic political upheavals. The decline of feudalism gave new importance to what would eventually become a rising middle class of merchants, shopkeepers, and professionals.

There was a sense of enthusiasm for expansion encouraged by Queen Elizabeth's emphasis on trade and travel to increase the nation's wealth. There were new ideas coming from students and teachers at the universities, and a sense of vitality in London that added to the energy and excitement.

During the Renaissance in England, guidance in spiritual matters was transferred from the Pope to the monarch, establishing the importance of individual conscience. Reformers began to look to education and the study of the classic works of Greece and Rome as alternatives to a single authority for matters of spiritual guidance.

On one hand, there were feelings of vitality, optimism, and national pride during the reign of Elizabeth. On the other hand, there was financial strain resulting from the prolonged trade wars with Spain. Toward the end of Elizabeth's reign there was also an increasing anxiety resulting from her having no heir apparent, a circumstance that would later plunge the nation into a disastrous civil war over the succession.

Shakespeare's life (1564–1616) straddled this period of hopeful change and the disillusionment that resulted from the corrupt reign of James I. Plays Shakespeare wrote during James I's reign include tragedies such as *Macbeth, Othello*, and *King Lear*.

WHAT WERE PEOPLE'S BELIEFS?

Not all people shared the same moral beliefs. Mercy, sin, pride, repentance, moderation, kingship, and God's power, however, were all central issues – important topics for sermons, for private conscience, and for literary exploration. The dramatic interest in Shakespeare's plays usually centres on the ways in which characters resolve spiritual, ethical, and political choices involving these issues. In both *Romeo and Juliet* and *The Merchant of Venice*, the issue of mercy is approached through a blending of Christian and classical ethics. In these and many other plays, Shakespeare portrayed the integration and balance of moral qualities as the basis of virtue and sound action.

"Providence," "fortune," and "chance" were important concepts to the Elizabethan people. Those who believed in Providence thought that God provided for and took care of those who trusted in Him. Protestants felt that Providence intervened directly when the winds changed in England's favour during the attempted invasion by the Spanish Armada. The evidence of providence was called fortune, a concept related to a person's fate. The image of fortune was often represented by a wheel upon which a person's career rose or fell.

Events manipulated by fortune were called "chance." Chance implies a sense of the randomness of life's incidents, which undermines any security we might have in predicting cause and effect. In *Hamlet*, we see Hamlet balance his desire for revenge with his concern that he may be misinterpreting providential "signs." In *Macbeth*, we see Macbeth realize that there are both good and evil implications in "chance": it may crown him King, but it may also expose his guilt when guardian angels "blow the horrid deed in every eye."

BIBLIOGRAPHY FOR SHAKESPEARE'S ENGLAND

The following references may be helpful to teachers and students if historical reading is desired.

Baugh, Albert C., Editor. *A Literary History of England.* Appleton-Century-Crofts, 1948

Bindoff, S.T. *Tudor England.* Penguin Books, 1969

Bowers, Fredson. *Elizabethan Revenge Tragedy.* Princeton University Press, 1966

Ferguson, Margaret F. *Rewriting the Renaissance.* University of Chicago Press, 1986

Frye, Roland Muskat. *Shakespeare and Christian Doctrine.* Princeton, University Press, 1963

Harrison, G.B. *Introducing Shakespeare.* Penguin Books, 1966

Holman, C. Hugh. *A Handbook to Literature.* Bobbs-Merrill Educational Publications, 1977

Joseph, B.L. *Shakespeare's Eden: The Commonwealth of England 1558–1629*, Blanford Press, 1971

Sandler, Robert, *Northrop Frye on Shakespeare*. Fitzhenry and Whiteside, 1986

Tillyard, Eustace M. *The Elizabethan World Picture*. Random House, 1959

Wilson, J. Dover. *Life in Shakespeare's England*. Cambridge University Press, 1962.

Approaches to *HBJ Shakespeare's Macbeth*

Teachers in student-centred classrooms where *Macbeth* is being studied should expect to receive many requests and experience many challenges from their students because the teachers are the resource people, the ones who have already studied the play. Students will seek guidance, clarification, and, sometimes even adjudication as they experience the play. As students' personal responses are further developed by their sharing with partners, dramatizing, and participating in group discussions and activities they will need to articulate their experiences to someone who is objective, knowledgeable, and sensitive to their needs.

There are several ways in which you might prepare for this challenging, interesting role. It is important to be familiar with the philosophy of the *HBJ Shakespeare* series and with its general format (see pages T6–T22). You should also feel familiar with and comfortable about the "To the Reader" and "Getting Started" sections of the student book (see pages 5–7) since they address the approach and major issues that students will encounter as they experience the play. *As it is neither practical nor desirable for students to complete all the activities presented throughout the text, you and your students could select those that best suit their needs, within the framework of available time for the study of this play and the objectives set for this study.*

You will probably find it useful to become acquainted with the background for *Macbeth* and with some of the many helpful resources related to it. *Macbeth*, more than most of Shakespeare's plays, is a product of its time. Obviously, pleasing both the patron of the King's Men, James I, and the London playgoing public was important to Shakespeare: the box office element is clearly evident throughout the play. The revision of history, at which the Tudors had excelled, was continued by the Stuarts; *Macbeth* reflects this. The play's stage history, with its popular additions, reworkings, and various interpretations, is of interest to many students. They usually enjoy the tales about the "curse of Macbeth" as well. This background material adapts well to research and independent study projects. Teachers need to familiarize themselves with these topics and resources so that they are able to offer support and guidance to students involved in these projects.

The material that follows provides a brief introduction to these topics, along with suggested references and resources.

BRIEF HISTORICAL BACKGROUND TO *MACBETH*

In medieval Scotland, the king's successor, or tanist, was usually named at the time of the king's accession. Tanistry, the Gaelic and Irish custom of electing the "worthiest kinsman," thus differed from the English system of primogeniture, in which the eldest son held the right of succession. From 859 to 1034 (Donald I to Malcolm II), no Scottish monarch was succeeded by his son or grandson; the usual sequence was brother of the king, followed by nephew of the king (that is, the son of the preceding king). For example, Kenneth I (843–859) was succeeded by his brother Donald I (859–863), who was succeeded by his nephew Constantine I (863–877), son of Kenneth. Constantine was, in turn, succeeded by his brother Aedh (877–878), and so on.

Malcolm II (1005–1034) succeeded his cousin Kenneth III (997–1005) and should have been followed by the heir of Kenneth. But it appears that Malcolm killed the legitimate successor and put his own grandson, Duncan, on the throne. Kenneth III's granddaughter, Grouch, however, upheld her family's claim on behalf of her son, Lulach. Grouch's second husband, Macbeth, then slew Duncan in battle (1040), was elected king, and ruled as the protector of the legitimate claims of Lulach. The Scots believed also, that, in his own right, Macbeth had a stronger claim to the throne than did Duncan. After a prosperous reign, Macbeth was killed in battle (1057) by Malcolm, son of Duncan. Malcolm III (called Canmore), who was only nine years old at the time of Duncan's death, reigned from 1058 to 1093, and died in battle.

It seems, then, that in tenth and eleventh-century Scotland the fate of most kings was to be killed in battle and probably by their successors, for the worthiest kinsman could well be the strongest kinsman.

With the rise of the Stuarts, primogeniture was firmly established. (In *Macbeth*, Shakespeare suppresses references to tanistry and emphasizes hereditary succession.) King James I of England was very proud of the fact that he was the ninth Stuart in lineal descent (as is shown in the "Show of Kings," Act 4, Scene 1 of *Macbeth*). The Stuarts traced their descent to a Breton family who were the stewards or seneschals of Dol, in Brittany. Walter, the son of the first immigrant to Scotland, Alan of Dol, was appointed steward of Scotland by David I. During the ensuing generations, these stewards (now Stewarts) acquired lands and titles in Scotland and England. Walter, the sixth Steward, married Princess Marjory, the daughter of Robert the Bruce. In 1371, their only son became Robert II, the founder of the royal Stewart line. The rights to the crowns of both

Scotland and England were merged in James V, for he was the son of James IV of Scotland and Margaret Tudor, daughter of Henry VII of England. It was James V's daughter Mary, Queen of Scots, who adopted the spelling "Stuart." On the death of Elizabeth I, Mary's son, James VI of Scotland, was proclaimed King James I of England.

If you, or some of your students, are interested in researching Scottish royal history further, the following chart, "The Kings of Scotland," will provide a starting point. Such turbulence surrounded royal deaths and successions that even a glance at the chart will help the interested student to grasp some of *Macbeth's* historical and Jacobean background.

EARLY KINGS OF SCOTLAND	DATES OF MONARCHY	RELATIONSHIP; DESTINY
Kenneth I MacAlpin	843–859	The first King of Scotland
Donald I	859–863	Brother of Kenneth I
Constantine I	863–877	Son of Kenneth I
Aedh	877–878	Brother of Constantine; murdered
Eochaid	878–889	Deposed
Giric	878–889	Regent for Eochaid
Donald II	889–900	
Constantine II	900–942	Abdicated
Malcolm I	942–954	Murdered
Indulf	954–962	
Dubh	962–967	Murdered
Culen	967–971	Murdered
Kenneth II	971–995	Murdered
Constantine III	995–997	Killed
Kenneth III	997–1005	Killed in battle by Malcolm II
Malcolm II	1005–1034	Son of Kenneth III
Duncan I	1034–1040	Grandson of Malcolm II; killed in battle by Macbeth
Macbeth	1040–1057	Killed in battle by Malcolm III
Lulach	1057–1058	Son of Grouch, Lady Macbeth; killed in battle
Malcolm III (Canmore)	1058–1093	Killed in battle

EARLY KINGS OF SCOTLAND	DATES OF MONARCHY	RELATIONSHIP; DESTINY
Donald III (Donald Bane)	1093–1094	Brother of Malcolm III; deposed
Duncan II	1094	Son of Malcolm III; murdered
Edmund	1094–1097	Son of Malcolm III; co-ruler; deposed
Donald III (Donald Bane)	1094–1097	Restored as co-ruler, then deposed
Edgar	1097–1107	Son of Malcolm III
Alexander I	1107–1124	Son of Malcolm III
David I	1124–1153	Son of Malcolm III
Malcolm IV	1153–1165	Grandson of David I
William I (The Lion)	1165–1214	Brother of Malcolm IV
Alexander II	1214–1249	Son of William I
Alexander III	1249–1286	Son of Alexander II; killed by a fall from his horse
Margaret of Norway	1286–1290	Grandaughter of Alexander III; died at sea
First Interregnum	1290–1292	
John Balliol	1292–1296	Abdicated
Second Interregnum	1296–1306	
Robert I (The Bruce)	1306–1329	
David II	1329–1371	Son of Robert Bruce; deposed 1332; returned 1340
Edward Balliol	1332–1338	Fled
Robert II Stewart	1371–1390	Nephew of David II; the first Stuart ruler
Robert III	1390–1406	
James I	1406–1437	Assassinated
James II	1437–1460	Accidentally killed in battle
James III	1460–1488	Killed during a civil rebellion
James IV	1488–1513	Married Margaret Tudor, daughter of King Henry VII of England; killed in battle

EARLY KINGS OF SCOTLAND	DATES OF MONARCHY	RELATIONSHIP; DESTINY
James V	1513–1542	
Mary, Queen of Scots	1542–1567	Daughter of James V; abdicated
James VI	1567–1625	James I of England, 1603

Subsequent monarchs ruled Great Britain.

HISTORICAL REVISIONISM AND SHAKESPEARE'S SOURCES

The advent of the royal Stewart line influenced the family to suggest their preference for a Scottish, rather than a Breton, ancestry. Historians seem to agree that, as a consequence, Banquo was "invented," a first or early reference to him occurring in Hector Boece's *Scotorum Historiae* (1527). Banquo was shown to be of royal stock descended from Kenneth MacAlpin, the first King of Scotland, and the mythical Fergus MacErc (who lived three hundred years before Christ). Banquo's son Fleance was shown to have married a Welsh princess, the daughter of King Griffith Llewelin, thereby granting to his descendants the additional privilege of descent from King Arthur of the Round Table. According to the "revised" history of Scotland, the Walter Steward who married the daughter of King Robert Bruce of Scotland was a third generation descendant of Fleance, making Banquo "the root and father of many kings."

By Shakespeare's time, Macbeth was seen as a murderer and tyrant, monster and usurper. In an early Scottish history, Wyntoun (about 1424) described Macbeth as a vicious murderer who killed his uncle and benefactor, Duncan, in response to prophecies uttered by "three weird sisters." Boece (1527) enlarged this story by showing that Banquo was also a recipient of prohecies. These stories were then further developed by Raphael Holinshed in his *Chronicles of England, Scotland, and Ireland* (1587), Holinshed becoming Shakespeare's major source. Relevant excerpts are printed in several editions of *Macbeth*: the New Variorum (Dover); the Arden (Methuen); and the Signet (New American Library).

Shakespeare used Holinshed's *Chronicles* selectively: he combined several stories, omitted much, and added more. The poet and dramatist was at work. But so was the pragmatist. The Lord

Chamberlain's Men had become, in 1603, the King's Men and Shakespeare and his fellow shareholders had been granted the status of Grooms of the Chamber. The number of court performances of their plays had more than doubled, and the remuneration for a court performance had doubled from 10 pounds to 20 pounds. Shakespeare was, therefore, well aware of the advantages of pleasing his royal patron. Since the Stuarts had chosen to trace their descent to Banquo – in fact to Arthur, – Shakespeare does not show Banquo as a co-murderer of Duncan. Nor does he allow Macbeth to have any valid claim to the throne or to have been other than a "butcher." Detailed evidence that Shakespeare wrote *Macbeth* with his royal patron in mind is presented by Henry H. Paul in *The Royal Play of Macbeth* (Macmillan, 1950). Arthur Melville Clark also presents much information on the play's contemporary background in *Murder Under Trust or the Topical Macbeth and other Jacobean Matters* (Scottish Academic Press, 1981).

CONTEMPORARY BACKGROUND

As E.M.W. Tillyard has pointed out, particularly in *The Elizabethan World Picture* (Penguin 1943, 1972) and in *Shakespeare's History Plays* (Penguin, 1944, 1969), the Elizabethans saw the universe as a perfect and unified creation of God, one in which everything had its place. This ordered world was a hierarchical one, a chain which ascended from the lowest form of inanimate substance, through vegtetable, animal, and human forms, to the highest archangel. Each section of the chain also contained its own hierarchy, so that every element was higher than another element: for example, the ruby was higher or nobler than the topaz, the oak than the bramble, the lion than the mouse. Further, each hierarchy had its corresponding leaders: the dolphin of the fish, the lion of the beasts, the head of the body, the king of the state, the sun of the stars, God of all the angels and of all the works of creation. Since the hierarchy of each section mirrored the others, all were influenced by disturbances in one. Thus, when King Duncan is murdered, reactions occur in other hierarchies, with unnatural disturbances in the heavens, and among the animals and birds.

The Elizabethan-Jacobean world regarded with horror the sin of regicide, seeing it as a violation of God's order and the destruction of His appointed representative. In fact, in his *Trew Law of Free Monarchies*, James pointed out that the anointed king, regardless of vicious or tyrannical qualities, must be obeyed and revered by his subjects.

James and his subjects were especially aware of the importance of order and control at this time. His undisputed succession in 1603 had relieved the anxieties of the English, who feared civil insurrection would follow the death of Elizabeth I. Then, in November 1605, the last-minute discovery of the Gunpowder Plot prevented the blowing-up of the king and destruction of parliament. A group of Roman Catholic gentlemen, frustrated by the anti-Catholic restrictions of the time, planned to kill the king and all his ministers, and then lead a great uprising of all English Catholics. In a cellar under the House of Lords they stored about two tons of gunpowder, planning to ignite it as James was opening parliament. However, the plot was leaked and Guy Fawkes was arrested as he entered the cellar – to this day in England he is burned in effigy on November 5. Many of the conspirators were executed, including the Superior of the Jesuits in England, Father Henry Garnet. During his trial, Garnet made reference to the Jesuit doctrine of equivocation, declaring that, under certain situations, one could swear to be telling the truth while retaining private mental reservations.

Shakespeare's references to equivocation, especially in the porter scene, (Act 2, Scene 3) likely met with a strong response from the king and his subjects. Other references that would please and flatter James occur in Act 4, Scene 3, at the court of the English King Edward. James had begun to "touch" for the "king's evil" or scrofula, the rite that is described by Malcolm in this scene. James also believed that he, like Edward, had the "heavenly gift of prophecy." In addition, James was proud of his connection to Edward the Confessor; Edward had died childless, but his cousin Edgar the Aetheling, grandson of King Edmund Ironside, should have succeeded him. Edgar's sister, Margaret, married Malcolm III (Canmore) of Scotland, and James was pleased to see himself as a descendant of the Saxon kings of England.

Another topical subject, witchcraft, would again appeal to both king and commoner. James had been involved in a Scottish witch trial, and believed that witches had tried to wreck the ship in which he was bringing his bride, Princess Anne of Denmark, to Scotland. He published his *Daemonologie in Forme of a Dialogue* in 1597 (Bodley Head, 1924) and continued to investigate alleged instances of witchcraft after his accession to the English throne. In 1604, England passed a statute for the suppression of witches, testifying to the general belief in their existence, tempered though it was by some doubts and scepticism (as in Reginald Scott's *Discoverie of Witchcraft*, 1584, Random House, 1930.)

THE STAGE HISTORY OF *MACBETH*

The first, or a very early, performance of *Macbeth* was before James I and King Christian IV of Denmark at Hampton Court, during Christian's visit to his sister, Queen Anne, in 1606.

The leading actor in Shakespeare's company, Richard Burbage, played Macbeth in early productions, including one in 1611 about which there is a detailed written description by Dr. Simon Forman, reprinted in the Arden, New Penguin, and New Variorum editions. During the Restoration, the play was substantially changed. Music, dancing, and spectacle were added, and some of Shakespeare's blunt epithets were modified (D'Avenant's version is reprinted in the New Variorum edition). In 1743, the actor David Garrick restored much of the original, but added a self-indulgent dying speech for Macbeth. It was not until the mid-nineteenth century that the play was again presented in its original First Folio form. Most major actors and actresses of the English-speaking world have played in *Macbeth*, presenting a fascinating variety of styles and interpretations. Two works that describe the play's stage history in some detail are A.C. Sprague's *Shakespeare and the Actors* (1944) and a full-length study by Dennis Bartholomeusz, *Macbeth and the Players* (Cambridge University Press, 1969). John D. Mitchell's *Macbeth Unjinxed* (Northwood Institute Press, 1985) is a description of a production from the director's point of view, and includes both the director's analysis of the meaning and purpose of each scene and the director's log.

The "curse" of *Macbeth* is another interesting facet of the play's stage history – in fact, the "curse," some believe, has extended to movies of the play and to productions of Verdi's opera, *Macbeth*. Theatre tradition recounts that during the play's first performance, probably before King James, the boy actor playing Lady Macbeth took ill and died, and Shakespeare himself had to take over the role. There is a long list of actors who have died or been injured during performances, of accidents with scenery, of problems such as fires and bomb threats in the theatres, and of failed or unsuccessful productions. A recent example of the "curse" at work occurred in January, 1988, when a voice coach fell to his death from a top balcony of the New York Metropolitan Opera during a production of Verdi's opera. Actors do not say the word "Macbeth" when the play is in rehearsal: the play is "The Scottish Play," and its characters are "The Thane" and "The Lady." Richard Huggett's *Supernatural on Stage: Ghosts and Superstitions of the Theatre* (Toplinger, 1975) has a chapter on the "curse," there is an amusing short article by Charles W. Yerger on his production of the play, "Macbeth: A Memoir," in *English Journal*, March 1983, and the curse is the focus for Ngaio Marsh's mystery novel *Light Thickens* (Fontana Collins, 1982.)

Probably the most reliable and accessible film version of *Macbeth* is the video in the BBC-TV series, *The Shakespeare Plays*, although Nicol Williamson's Macbeth may seem a little histrionic to some viewers. Another dependable film is George Schaeffer's version of 1960, with Maurice Evans and Judith Anderson. Roman Polanski's 1971 movie is popular with students; the youth of the Macbeths (Jon Finch and Francesa Annis) is a convincing element, and the symbols are memorable. However, the film's blood and violence may cause offence.

Attempts to change the play's setting in time and place include the 1955 movie *Joe Macbeth*, set in Chicago's gangland, and the 1957 Japanese *Throne of Blood* (Kumonosu-Djo) by Kurosawa, set amongst medieval Japanese samurai.

Andrew M. McLean's *Shakespeare: Annotated Bibliographies and Media Guide for Teachers* (National Council of Teachers of English, 1977) provides a bibliography of reviews and articles on the Kurosawa, Schaeffer, and Polanski films, as well as on Orson Welles' 1948 film. This work also lists the sources for these films as well as other audio-visual resources for the teaching of Shakespeare in general and *Macbeth* in particular.

Complete recordings of the play have been made by the Old Vic Company (RCA-Victor), The Marlowe Society (Argo), and Caedmon-SRS.

PRESENTING *MACBETH* IN A CONDENSED TIME PERIOD

Macbeth, at approximately 2000 lines, is Shakespeare's shortest tragedy; *Hamlet*, in comparison, has approximately 4000 lines. In fact, of all the plays, only *Comedy of Errors* is shorter. While Shakespeare may have been conscious of the fact that James I disliked long plays and often left before a play ended, there are other reasons for the play's brevity. *Macbeth* lacks a subplot, so the action is Macbeth-centred: we watch the commission of a crime and its consequences on the murderer. In the few scenes where Macbeth is not physically on stage, he remains the centre of our focus and consciousness. The movement is rapid, creating the feeling in the audience that the whole play takes place in only a few days. (There are, in fact, about nine days accounted for in the play, although historically Macbeth's rule spanned seventeen years.) The rapid pace of events is further emphasized by the large number of scene changes – from heath, to battlefield, to castle, and so on – this technique being particularly effective in the fast-moving battle scenes of Act 5. *Macbeth* presents 29 scenes, compared with *Hamlet's* 20 and *Othello's* 15. The poetry of the play is particularly compressed and concentrated, characterized by complex metaphors and recurrent and unifying imagery. Nevertheless, it is possible to condense the play further, or to concentrate class study on specific scenes if your teaching time is limited.

Some scenes may be omitted. Most modern productions leave out the Hecate scenes (Act 3, Scene 5 and a small section of Act 4, Scene 1) because there is strong evidence that these were pre-First Folio interpolations, partly as a consequence of the popularity of Middleton's play *The Witch* (reprinted in the New Variorum edition), which was probably written some time between 1610 and 1620. Such an omission changes nothing in the play, either in study or performance.

Some productions either omit or shorten the Porter scene (Act 2, Scene 3). Arguments against this omission include the practical one that the actor playing Macbeth needs time to wash his hands and change his clothes (and take a break, after one of drama's most harrowing scenes). The audience, too, needs some relief from the intensity of the murder and its imminent discovery. (Thomas de Quincy's famous essay, "On the Knocking at the Gate in *Macbeth*," describes the effects of this scene on the audience and he would doubtless argue for its retention.) The thematic arguments against the omission centre on the scene's focus on equivocation. Nevertheless, in the classroom one could show a film version of the scene, or play a recording. The students can enjoy the grim humour without looking at topical references. Then the study would begin with Macduff's "Is thy master stirring?"

Another omission could be part or all of the scene set in England (Act 4, Scene 3), the play's longest scene. Even director John Mitchell, who argues strongly in *Macbeth Unjinxed* for the scene's retention, admits that it is difficult to stage. In both the testing of Macduff and the description of the piety of King Edward there is much theoretical talk and no action: the scene often "drags" on stage. Thematically, of course, the scene is vital; we need to see the forces of good assembling, to learn, by antithesis, what a king *should* be. But for classroom study, you could well show the class one of the film versions of the scene and move immediately to Act 5.

There are several other possible brief omissions: the conversation between Ross and the Old Man (Act 2, Scene 4), the conversation between Lennox and another Lord (Act 3, Scene 6), and the conversations between Lady Macduff and Ross, and Lady Macduff and her son (Act 4, Scene 2, lines 1–64). There are, of course, strong reasons for the retention of these scenes as well.

A very concentrated study is possible if one focusses on Macbeth before and after each murder and the death of his wife.

The Murder of Duncan

- The first soliloquy (actually, an "aside"), "Two truths are told . . ." (Act 1, Scene 3, lines 137–161)

- The second aside, "The Prince of Cumberland . . ." (Act 1, Scene 4, lines 55–60)

- The second soliloquy, "If it were done . . ." (Act 1, Scene 7, lines 1–28)

- The third soliloquy, "Is this a dagger . . ." (Act 2, Scene 1, lines 40–71)

- The conversation with Lady Macbeth after Duncan's murder, "I have done the deed . . ." (Act 2, Scene 2, lines 18–93)

The Murder of Banquo

- The fourth soliloquy, "To be thus is nothing . . ." (Act 3, Scene 1, lines 52–77)

- Conversation with Lady Macbeth before Banquo's murder, "We have scotch'd the snake . . ." (Act 3, Scene 2, lines 15–61)

- Asides when the murderers reveal that Fleance has escaped, "Then comes my fit again . . ." (Act 3, Scene 4, lines 24–38)

- Macbeth's words to the ghost of Banquo, "Thou canst not say I did it . . ." (Act 3, Scene 4, lines 63–64, 83–87, 113–131, 151–155)

Murder of the Macduffs

- First suggestion that Macduff is next on the list: conversation with Lady Macbeth, "How say'st thou, that Macduff denies his person . . ." (Act 3, Scene 4, lines 158–175)

- Macbeth's reaction to the prophecies, "Then live, Macduff . . ." (Act 4, Scene 1, lines 88–92)

- Aside, "Time, thou anticipatest my dread exploits . . ." (Act 4, Scene 1, lines 158–170)

- Final words to Macduff, "Of all men else . . ." (Act 5, Scene 8, lines 5–39)

Lady Macbeth's Death

- The fifth soliloquy, "This push will cheer me ever . . ." (Act 5, Scene 3, lines 22–31)

- The sixth soliloquy, "I have almost forgot the taste of fears . . ." (Act 5, Scene 5, lines 10–30)

Similarly, a concentrated study of Lady Macbeth could address a few key speeches. Students might try to decide just how strong a woman she is at the beginning of the play, look at what her various displays of strength and encouragement cost her, consider her motivation, and discuss the inevitability of her final days and her death. You could focus on Lady Macbeth in the following passages:

- The first soliloquy, "Glamis thou art, and Cawdor . . ." (Act 1, Scene 5, lines 14–62)

- Her appeal to Macbeth's manhood, "Was the hope drunk . . ." (Act 1, Scene 7, lines 38–92)

- Her need for liquor, "That which hath made them drunk . . ." (Act 2, Scene 2, lines 1–17)

- Her practicality and control, "Who was it thus that cried . . ." (Act 2, Scene 2, lines 57–91)

- The second (very short) soliloquy, "Nought's had, all's spent . . ." (Act 3, Scene 2, lines 6–9)

- Her weariness at the end of the banquet scene, "Almost at odds with morning . . ." (Act 3, Scene 4, lines 156–175)

- The sleepwalking scene (Act 5, Scene 1)

This focussed study on each or both of the Macbeths and the destruction of their relationship and lives should lead students into thematic issues as the destruction of other people and of nature; the contrast between appearance and reality; and the constant need for awareness of what *is* real and what only *appears* real.

A SELECTION OF SUGGESTED
CLASSROOM RESOURCES

Humour

Students always enjoy satirical or light-hearted spoofs of school texts; the following seem most enjoyed if they are read aloud:

Armour, Richard, "Macbeth," *Twisted Tales from Shakespeare*. Signet, 1957.

Full of groan-inspiring puns.

Bazagonov, M.S., "Macbeth," *Shakespeare in the Red*. Flegon Press, 1964.
  Amusing in parts. The story is told from a communist point of view.
Thurber, James, "The Macbeth Murder Mystery," in *My World – and Welcome to It*. Harcourt Brace Jovanovich, 1937, 1965.

Rhymed Versions

Greenwell, Bill, "Macbeth," and Holtby, Mary, "Macbeth," in Parrott, E.O., ed., *How to Become Ridiculously Well-Read in One Evening: A Collection of Literary Encapsulations*. Viking, 1985.
Smith, Horace and James, "Macbeth," Zaranka, William, ed., *The Brand-X Anthology of Poetry: A Parody Anthology* (Burnt Norton Edition). Apple-Wood Books, 1981.

Related Themes

The student who loves to read may be interested in exploring some of the play's ideas and themes in other forms and variations.

The large body of Faust-inspired material deals with the giving of the soul and/or body to evil, in return for certain promised outcomes. One of the earliest versions is Christopher Marlowe's tragedy *Doctor Faustus* (believed to have been written between 1588 and 1592). Goethe began a long line of Faust-inspired German literature, perhaps the most accessible (but for mature students) being Klaus Mann's *Mephisto* (Penguin, 1977, 1983). Somewhat simpler North American versions include Stephen Vincent Benet's 1937 short story, "The Devil and Daniel Webster," and W.O. Mitchell's play, *The Black Bonspiel of Wullie MacCrimmon*, 1965.

Works that deal with the protagonist's belief in prophecies include Oscar Wilde's story, "Lord Arthur Savile's Crime: A Study of Duty," and Eugene O'Neill's 1920 play, *The Emperor Jones*.

Described as a "vicious satire," Barbara Garson's 1966 play, *Macbird*, casts Lyndon Johnson as "Macbird," John F. Kennedy as Duncan, and Robert Kennedy as Malcolm-Macduff, and features such prophecies as "All Hail, Macbird, that Shalt be President." A mature student who is interested in American politics of this period might find this a stimulating independent study project.

Selected Criticism

There is, of course, a large body of *Macbeth* criticism. One of the most useful and accessible is Terence Hawkes, ed., *Twentieth Century Interpretations of Macbeth: A Collection of Critical Essays* (Prentice-Hall, 1977). In the same category, but with fewer specifically *Macbeth* essays and excerpts is Laurence Lerner, ed., *Shakespeare's Tragedies: An Anthology of Modern Criticism*. As well as excerpts from Holinshed's *Chronicles*, the Signet edition of the play contains some useful criticism. Volume XIX of the *Shakespeare Survey* is devoted to *Macbeth* (Kenneth Muir, ed., 1966). If more detailed reading appeals, the two "classics" which form the springboard for much subsequent and contemporary criticism are A.C. Bradley's *Shakespearean Tragedy: Lectures on Hamlet, Othello, King Lear, Macbeth* (Macmillan, 1904, paperback 1974) and Caroline Spurgeon's *Shakespeare's Imagery and What It Tells Us* (Cambridge University Press, 1935). Finally, John Russell Brown's *Shakespeare: The Tragedy of Macbeth*, written for senior students, describes the play's background, then gives brief and perceptive explanations and analyses of each scene.

REFERENCES CITED

Amour, Richard, *Twisted Tales from Shakespeare*. Signet/The New American Library of Canada, 1957.

Barnet, Sylvan, ed., *The Tragedy of Macbeth*. Signet/The New American Library of Canada, 1963.

Bartholomeusz, Dennis, *Macbeth and the Players*. Cambridge University Press, 1969. Published in paperback 1978.

Bazagonov, M.S. *Shakespeare in the Red: Tales from Shakespeare by a Soviet Lamb*. Flegon Press, 1964.

Benet, Stephen Vincent, "The Devil and Daniel Webster." 1937.

Bradley, A.C., *Shakespearean Tragedy: Lectures on Hamlet, Othello, King Lear, Macbeth*. Macmillan, 1904. Published in Macmillan Student Editions, 1974.

Brown, John Russell, *Shakespeare: The Tragedy of Macbeth*. Edward Arnold, 1963.

Clark, Arthur Melville, *Murder under Trust or The Topical Macbeth*. Scottish Academic Press, 1981.

De Quincey, Thomas, "On the Knocking at the Gate in *Macbeth*." 1823.

Furness, Horace Howard Jr., *A New Variorum Edition of Shakespeare: Macbeth*. Dover, 1963.

Garson, Barbara, *Macbird*. Grove Press, 1966, 1967.

Hawkes, Terence, ed., *Twentieth Century Interpretations of Macbeth: A Collection of Critical Essays*. Prentice-Hall, 1977.

Huggett, Richard, "The Curse of *Macbeth*: Its Origins, Background, and History," *Supernatural on Stage: Ghosts and Superstitions of the Theatre*. Toplinger, 1975.

Hunter, G.K., ed., *Macbeth*, The New Penguin Shakespeare. Penguin, 1967.

Lerner, Laurence, ed., *Shakespeare's Tragedies: An Anthology of Modern Criticism*. The Penguin Shakespeare Library. Penguin, 1968.

McLean, Andrew, M., *Shakespeare: Annotated Bibliographies and Media Guide for Teachers*. National Council of Teachers of English, 1980.

Mann, Klaus, *Mephisto*. Translated by Robin Smyth. Penguin, 1977, 1983.

Marlowe, Christopher, *The Tragical History of the Life and Death of Doctor Faustus*. c. 1588–1592.

Marsh, Ngaio, *Light Thickens*. Fontana Collins, 1983.

Mitchell, John D., *Macbeth Unjinxed*. Northwood Institute Press, 1985.

Mitchell, W.O., *The Black Bonspiel of Wullie MacCrimmon*. 1965.

Muir, Kenneth, *Macbeth* (Arden Edition). Methuen, 1951. Published in University Paperback, 1972.

Muir, Kenneth, ed., *Shakespeare Survey*, Vol. XIX. Cambridge University Press, 1966.

O'Neill, Eugene, *The Emperor Jones*. 1920.

Parrott, E.O., *How to Become Ridiculously Well-Read in One Evening: A Collection of Literary Encapsulations*. Viking, 1985.

Paul, Henry N., *The Royal Play of Macbeth*. Macmillan, 1950.

Sprague, Arthur Colby, *Shakespeare and the Actors: The Stage Business in His Plays 1660–1905*. Harvard University Press, 1944, 1948.

Spurgeon, Caroline F.E., *Shakespeare's Imagery and What it Tells Us*. Cambridge University Press, 1935.

Thurber, James, *My World – and Welcome to It*. Harcourt Brace Jovanovich, 1937, 1965.

Tillyard, E.M.W., *The Elizabethan World Picture*. Penguin, 1943, 1972.

Tillyard, E.M.W., *Shakespeare's History Plays*. Penguin, 1944, 1986.

Yerger, Charles W., "Macbeth: A Memoir," *English Journal*. The National Council of Teachers of English, March 1983.

Zaranka, William, ed., *The Brand-X Anthology of Poetry. Burnt Norton Edition*. Apple-Wood Books, 1981.

MACBETH

HBJ SHAKESPEARE

MACBETH

edited by
Margaret Kortes

Harcourt Brace Jovanovich, Canada

Toronto Orlando San Diego London Sydney

HBJ Shakespeare: Series Editor, Ken Roy

Canadian Cataloguing in Publication Data

Shakespeare, William, 1564–1616
  Macbeth

(HBJ Shakespeare)
For use in high schools.
ISBN 0-7747-1270-8

I. Kortes, Margaret. II. Title. III. Series.

PR2823.A2K67 1988   822.3′3   C88-093589-8

88 89 90 91 92   5 4 3 2 1

Editorial Director: Murray Lamb
Senior Editor: Lydia Fletcher
Project Editor: Elynor Kagan
Designer: Michael van Elsen
Illustrators: Marika and Laszlo Gal
Cover Illustrators: Marika and Laszlo Gal
Typesetter: Q Composition
Printed in Canada by Friesen Printers

Acknowledgments

The editor and publisher acknowledge the consultant
listed below for her contribution to the development of this
program:

Leuba Bailey
English Teacher, Daniel McIntyre Collegiate, Winnipeg School
Division, Winnipeg, Manitoba

To the Reader

Taking a few moments to think and sometimes write about
your responses to a literary work helps you to feel comfortable
and familiar with it. As you read, watch, or listen to *Macbeth*,
write down ideas that interest, puzzle, or bother you. You
could sketch images or ideas or write down quotations that
you find particularly striking. You may discover that you
recall similar experiences to those characters in the play are
having and want to make note of these similarities.

Your responses are an important aspect of your experience
of the play. This text provides you with opportunities to share
your responses with partners, small groups, and/or the
whole class. You may find yourself becoming one of the
characters, an actor, director, film-maker, or media representative, and sharing your responses to the play from
these different perspectives.

HBJ Macbeth is designed to help you experience the world
of the play. The map on page 4 shows you the locations
of castles, battlefields, and the various thanedoms, or lands
controlled by the Scottish nobles, at the time of *Macbeth*.
Illustrations of scenes and characters that you will encounter throughout the text help you visualize the settings and
action. To assist you in understanding each scene, a brief
note provides you with an outline of events in the scene.
The questions that precede scenes give you the opportunity
to think, talk, or write about aspects of your own experience
that may be relevant to the scenes. Activities following scenes
and acts allow you to review your responses to the characters and events, placing them in a broader perspective. As
you complete selected activities, you will find that characters such as Macbeth, Lady Macbeth, Banquo, and Macduff
have passions, ambitions, hopes, temptations, and fears just
as you have. You will probably also find that they have
something to contribute to your understanding of humanity.

1

Getting Started

Although you may not yet have read or seen *Macbeth*, you will soon recognize some familiar conflicts and issues, for you have seen them on television and in films, you have read about them in newspapers and magazines. In the play, there are conflicts between heroism and villainy, good and evil, loyalty and treachery, ambition and morality. In addition, there are conflicting loyalties – to king, country, family. You will recognize the murder mystery theme as well as the murderer's attempts to conceal and lie and cover up, as his fear and desperation grow. You may recognize the ideas that life without love, friendship, and self-respect is meaningless or that guilt can be overwhelming.

We have all become familiar with the consequences of political upheaval, civil and foreign wars, with the grim reality that innocent people – especially children – suffer during such times. Even in our own times, we have seen that civil liberties such as freedom of speech and freedom from arbitrary arrest or execution are quickly eroded by dictatorships.

Even though the play deals with much that is familiar, it leads you to consider some new and unusual ideas, and to learn more about yourself and others. Perhaps you may not expect that a murderer would have a vivid and poetic imagination or that he would, even in defeat, demonstrate conscience and courage. You might not expect that an apparently strong, practical, and determined woman would act in such contradiction to her real nature that madness and violent suicide are the consequence.

Before you begin your experience of the play, decide how you can best keep track of your different responses. You may wish to keep separate your private journal responses from those you plan to share with your classmates and/or teacher. Your answers to general questions could be written in a notebook and longer written responses, such as letters or news reports, could be kept in a writing folder. Ideas on staging the play could be written in a director's log.

To focus your response to *Macbeth*, you might want to think, write or talk about some of the following issues. They will lead you to important perceptions – of the play's characters, of yourself, and of others.

2

1. Think of some people you know or have read about who are/were ambitious. Have their ambitions led to a positive or negative result? Are ambitions sometimes destructive? Explain.

2. What is your understanding of the philosophy, "the end justifies the means"? Give examples of situations in which you would agree and disagree with this philosophy.

3. Would assassination or civil war ever be a justifiable response to rule by tyranny? What would you do if the leader of your country became a vicious tyrant?

4. Are a citizen's first responsibilites to family, political leader, or country?

5. Describe some examples of what you think is evil behaviour. How should evil behaviour be dealt with?

6. If you suspected, but had no evidence, that a friend of yours had committed a crime, what would you do?

7. How do you deal with your fears? How might you help others to deal with theirs? What are some of the effects that fear can have on people?

8. Describe a time you experienced insomnia (lack of sleep). What did you do about it? What are some of the effects that insomnia can have on people who suffer from it?

9. Describe a woman who best represents your idea of "womanliness." Describe a man who best depicts "manliness." Are there any similarities between the two descriptions? Why or why not?

10. Explain what you think an "ideal" marriage would be.

11. Describe a situation in which you or someone you know has been deceived by appearances. How might you advise someone to guard against this trap?

12. What do you want most from life? What are you prepared to do to attain it?

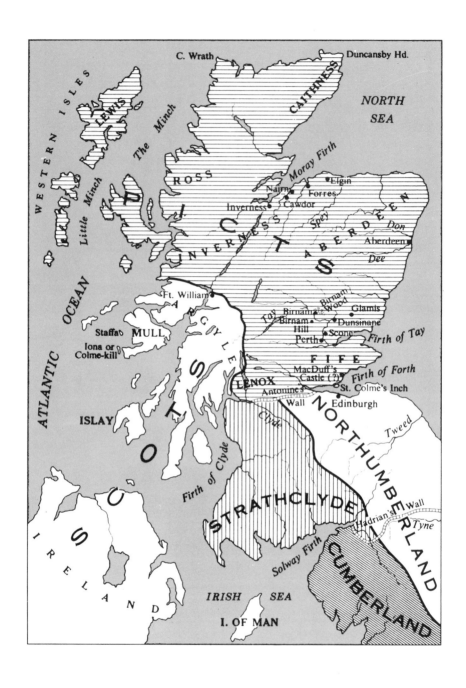

Dramatis Personae

(Characters in the Play)

Duncan, King of Scotland
Malcolm
Donalbain } his sons
Macbeth
Banquo } generals of the King's army
Macduff
Lennox
Ross
Menteith } noblemen of Scotland
Angus
Caithness
Fleance, son to Banquo
Siward, Earl of Northumberland, general of the English forces
Young Siward, his son
Seyton, an officer attending on Macbeth
Boy, son to Macduff
An English Doctor
A Scotch Doctor
A Sergeant
A Porter
An Old Man
Lady Macbeth
Lady Macduff
Gentlewoman attending on Lady Macbeth
Hecate
Three Witches
Apparitions
**Lords, Gentlemen, Officers, Soldiers, Murderers, Attendants,
    and Messengers**
Scene: Scotland; England

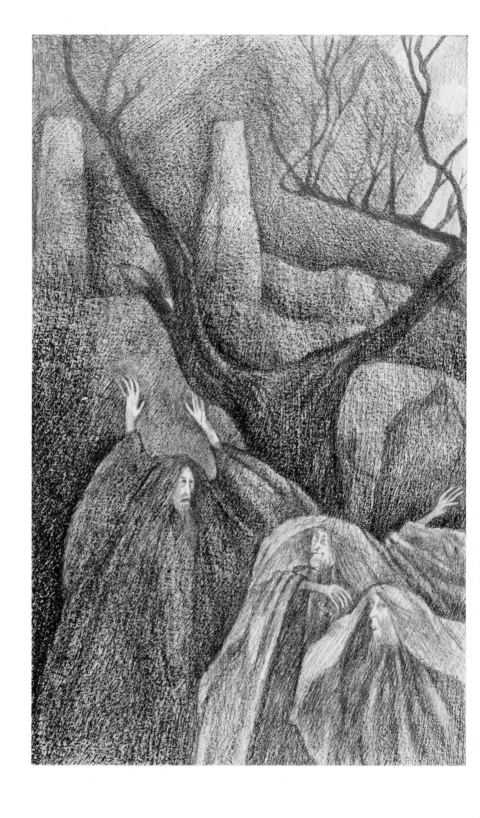

Act 1, Scene 1

In this scene . . .

Set in medieval Scotland, the play opens in an isolated and wild place. Amid thunder and lightning, three witches enter. They reveal characteristics traditionally associated with witchcraft: they know in advance the outcome of a civil war that is being fought in Scotland, and they know when and where they will encounter Macbeth, one of the generals. The witches are called away by their companion spirits and they fly off into the murky air.

Scene location—*desert:* wild and uninhabited

3   *hurlyburly:* uproar, turmoil, confusion, especially relating to battle or rebellion

9-10   *Graymalkin and Paddock:* the witches' demon companions or familiar spirits, who are calling the witches. Graymalkin is a cat, Paddock a toad.

10   *anon:* I'm coming immediately

Act 1, Scene 1

*A desert place. Thunder and
lightning.*

Enter three Witches.

First Witch: When shall we three meet again
  In thunder, lightning, or in rain?
Second Witch: When the hurlyburly's done.
  When the battle's lost and won.
Third Witch: That will be ere the set of sun.   5
First Witch: Where the place?
Second Witch: Upon the heath.
Third Witch: There to meet with Macbeth.
First Witch: I come, Graymalkin.
All: Paddock calls;—anon.   10
  Fair is foul, and foul is fair,
  Hover through the fog and filthy air.

                 [*Witches vanish*]

Act 1, Scene 1: Activities

1. How would you stage this scene? What methods would you use to create thunder, lightning, darkness, and fog? What other special effects would you include? In groups, discuss your ideas.

2. At the end of the scene, the three witches say, "Fair is foul, and foul is fair." What do you think they mean?

For the next scene . . .

Who are your heroes? What qualities or characteristics do they possess that make them heroic?

Act 1, Scene 2

In this scene . . .

At King Duncan's camp, some distance from the actual fighting, the king, his sons, and attendants are given the latest report from the battlefield. A wounded soldier praises the bravery of the two generals Macbeth and Banquo, and describes their victory over the traitor Macdonwald, followed by their defence against Sweno, the King of Norway, whose forces have come to the aid of the rebels. The Thane of Ross arrives to announce the victory of Macbeth and Banquo over Sweno, who has been assisted by another traitor, the Thane of Cawdor. King Duncan orders Cawdor's immediate execution and transfers his title to Macbeth. All the reports stress the violent and bloody nature of the war.

Stage direction—*Alarum within:* A trumpet sounds off-stage.
The trumpet signals the soldiers to arm themselves.

2   *As seemeth by his plight:* judging from his condition

5-6   *fought/ 'Gainst my captivity:* saved me from being taken prisoner

7   *broil:* tumult, battle

10-11   *As two . . . their art:* Just as two exhausted swimmers cling to each other and so make it impossible for either to survive.

12   *for to that:* the proof of it is that

13-14   *the multiplying villainies . . . upon him:* It is as if increasing numbers of insects (such as lice) are swarming all over his body; he is becoming increasingly evil.

14   *the western isles:* the Hebrides, a group of islands off the west coast of Scotland (see map, page 4)

15   *kerns and gallowglasses:* troops from the Hebrides. Kerns were lightly armed foot soldiers; gallowglasses were more heavily armed mounted soldiers, wielding axes.

16-17   *And fortune . . . rebel's whore:* Fortune appeared at first to favour the rebel Macdonwald just as a prostitute appears to favour a man for a short time but does not remain with him.

16   *all's too weak:* neither Macdonwald nor Fortune could withstand Macbeth

19   *steel:* sword

21   *minion:* darling, favourite

21   *the slave:* Macdonwald

23   *Which ne'er shook hands . . . to him:* Macbeth did not observe the usual courtesies of medieval warfare.

24   *unseam'd him from the nave to the chaps:* cut him open from the navel to the jaws

26   *cousin:* Macbeth and Duncan are first cousins; the word also indicates kinship in general.

Scene 2

*A camp near Forres. Alarum
within.*

*Enter King Duncan, Malcolm,
Donalbain, Lennox, with
Attendants, meeting a bleeding
Soldier.*

Duncan: What bloody man is that? He can report,
  As seemeth by his plight, of the revolt
  The newest state.
Malcolm: This is the sergeant
  Who like a good and hardy soldier fought   5
  'Gainst my captivity. Hail, brave friend!
  Say to the king the knowledge of the broil
  As thou didst leave it.
Soldier: Doubtful it stood;
  As two spent swimmers, that do cling together   10
  And choke their art. The merciless Macdonwald—
  Worthy to be a rebel, for to that
  The multiplying villainies of nature
  Do swarm upon him—from the western isles
  Of kerns and gallowglasses is supplied;   15
  And fortune, on his damned quarrel smiling,
  Show'd like a rebel's whore: but all's too weak;
  For brave Macbeth—well he deserves that name—
  Disdaining fortune, with his brandish'd steel,
  Which smoked with bloody execution,   20
  Like valour's minion carved out his passage
  Till he faced the slave;
  Which ne'er shook hands, nor bade farewell to him,
  Till he unseam'd him from the nave to the chaps,
  And fix'd his head upon our battlements.   25
Duncan: O valiant cousin! worthy gentleman!

27-30   *As whence the sun . . . Discomfort swells:* Just as the rising of the sun is sometimes followed by storms which begin in the east, so Macbeth's victory gave way to a new assault on his forces.

33   *the Norweyan lord, surveying vantage:* Sweno, King of Norway, seeing an opportunity

40   *sooth:* the truth

41   *double cracks:* a double load of ammunition

44   *Except they meant to bathe in reeking wounds:* whether they intended to bathe in blood

45   *memorize another Golgotha:* make this battlefield as famous as Golgotha or Calvary. This was the site of Christ's crucifixion and of the execution of criminals, and was known as "the place of the skull".

47-48   *So well thy words . . . honour both:* Both your words and your wounds suggest your honour.

50   *thane:* a Scottish noble equivalent in rank to an English earl

56-59   *From Fife . . . fan our people cold:* The Norwegian forces have invaded Fife and the people are fearful. (See map, page 4.)

61   *dismal:* disastrous

62   *Bellona's bridegroom:* Mars, the Roman god of war (Bellona was the Roman goddess of war.) Ross is referring to Macbeth.

62   *lapp'd in proof:* wearing tested and proven armour

63-64   *Confronted him with . . . arm 'gainst arm:* Macbeth faced the King of Norway with equal valour and equal arms.

Soldier: As whence the sun 'gins his reflection
   Shipwrecking storms and direful thunders break,
   So from that spring whence comfort seem'd to come,
   Discomfort swells, Mark, King of Scotland, mark: 30
   No sooner justice had, with valour arm'd,
   Compell'd these skipping kernes to trust their heels,
   But the Norweyan lord, surveying vantage,
   With furbish'd arms and new supplies of men,
   Began a fresh assault.   35
Duncan: Dismay'd not this
   Our captains, Macbeth and Banquo?
Soldier: Yes;
   As sparrows, eagles, or the hare, the lion.
   If I say sooth, I must report they were   40
   As cannons overcharged with double cracks;
   So they doubly redoubled strokes upon the foe:
   Except they meant to bathe in reeking wounds,
   Or memorize another Golgotha,
   I cannot tell—   45
   But I am faint, my gashes cry for help.
Duncan: So well thy words become thee as thy wounds;
   They smack of honour both. Go get him surgeons.
                         [*Exit Soldier, attended*]
   Who comes here?
   [*Enter Ross*]
Malcolm: The worthy thane of Ross.   50
Lennox: What haste looks through his eyes! So should he
   look
   That seems to speak things strange.
Ross: God save the king!
Duncan: Whence camest thou, worthy thane?   55
Ross: From Fife, great king;
   Where the Norweyan banners flout the sky
   And fan our people cold. Norway himself,
   With terrible numbers,
   Assisted by that most disloyal traitor   60
   The thane of Cawdor, began a dismal conflict:
   Till that Bellona's bridegroom, lapp'd in proof,
   Confronted him with self-comparisons,
   Point against point, rebellious arm 'gainst arm,

69   *craves composition:* begs for terms of a truce

70   *deign:* allow

71   *Saint Colme's Inch:* an island in the Firth of Forth, an inlet of the North Sea which divides Scotland and Norway. The island is also known as Saint Columba's Island or Inchcolm. (See map, page 4.)

73-74   *deceive our bosom interest:* betray our affection, close friendship

74   *present:* immediate

Curbing his lavish spirit: and, to conclude,   65
The victory fell on us.
Duncan: Great happiness!
Ross: That now
Sweno, the Norway's king, craves composition;
Nor would we deign him burial of his men   70
Till he disbursed, at Saint Colme's inch,
Ten thousand dollars to our general use.
Duncan: No more that thane of Cawdor shall deceive
Our bosom interest: go, pronounce his present death,
And with his former title greet Macbeth.   75
Ross: I'll see it done.
Duncan: What he hath lost, noble Macbeth hath won.
                                        [*Exeunt*]

Act 1, Scene 2: Activities

1. From the descriptions given of Macbeth, do you admire him?

2. As a news reporter for a national television channel, you are covering the Scottish Civil War. You have been asked to prepare a five-minute report on the final day of battle for the evening newscast. With a partner, write your recorded commentary and describe the camera shots that would be included during this national news report. You may wish to make a video of your report to share with others.

3. You are an official in Duncan's court who has just heard the five-minute report described in #2. Write a description of your own reactions to the report and to the victorious general, the Thane of Macbeth.

4. Write the diary entry for King Duncan, as he reviews this eventful day. Take care to note his feelings about the traitors who have rebelled against him.

For the next scene . . .

Do you believe in fortune-telling? Do you read your horoscope? Why or why not?

Act 1, Scene 3

In this scene . . .

The witches gather in a bleak place, somewhere between the battlefield and Duncan's palace at Forres.
They report with delight the discomforts they have
been causing and then prepare a spell for Macbeth.
Macbeth and Banquo, who are on their way to Forres,
enter and are astonished to see the witches and to hear
what they have to say. The witches tell Macbeth that
he will become Thane of Glamis, Thane of Cawdor,
and King of Scotland. Banquo asks the witches to tell
him about his future but the answers he receives are
filled with paradox. The witches prophesy that Banquo will be both lesser and greater than Macbeth, not
so happy but happier, not king himself but father of
a line of kings. The witches vanish. Banquo is sceptical
about the prophecies, but Macbeth believes them.
The first of his prophecies has already been fulfilled –
the death of his father has made him Thane of Glamis.
In addition, Ross and Angus arrive shortly after the
witches have disappeared to tell Macbeth that the king
has named him Thane of Cawdor. Macbeth thinks
immediately of murdering Duncan, which would open
the way for the third prophecy to come true, even
though he is horrified by his own idea.

2   *killing swine:* It was believed that witches were especially vengeful against pigs.

5   *mounch'd:* munched

6   *quoth:* said

7   *Aroint thee:* begone, go away; *rump-fed ronyon:* overfed, fat-bottomed, mangy creature

8   *Aleppo:* an important trading city in northern Syria; *master:* captain; *the Tiger:* a common Elizabethan name for a ship.

9   *sieve:* It was believed that witches could sail on the sea in a sieve.

10   *like a rat without a tail:* Witches could transform themselves into other shapes, usually animals. In this case the tail would be missing, perhaps because there is no part of a human form to change into a tail in the way that hands and feet could be transformed into paws.

12   *I'll give thee a wind:* Witches were believed to be sellers of winds.

15   *I myself have all the other:* I have enough other winds.

18   *shipman's card:* navigator's compass chart

21   *pent-house lid:* eye-lid. A pent-house was a sloping roof attached to a larger building.

22   *forbid:* cursed

23   *se'nnights:* a week; *nine:* a mystical or magical number favoured by witches

24   *dwindle, peak, and pine:* waste away

25   *bark:* ship. It was believed that witches could not cause a ship to be wrecked; they could only make the voyage perilous.

Scene 3

A *heath. Thunder.*

Enter the three Witches.

First Witch: Where hast thou been, sister?
Second Witch: Killing swine.
Third Witch: Sister, where thou?
First Witch: A sailor's wife had chestnuts in her lap,
 And mounch'd, and mounch'd, and mounch'd.   5
  "Give me," quoth I:
 "Aroint thee, witch!" the rump-fed ronyon cries.
 Her husband's to Aleppo gone, master o' the Tiger:
 But in a sieve I'll thither sail,
 And like a rat without a tail,   10
 I'll do, I'll do, and I'll do.
Second Witch: I'll give thee a wind.
First Witch: Thou'rt kind.
Third Witch: And I another.
First Witch: I myself have all the other;   15
 And the very ports they blow,
 All the quarters that they know
 I' the shipman's card.
 I'll drain him dry as hay:
 Sleep shall neither night nor day   20
 Hang upon his pent-house lid;
 He shall live a man forbid:
 Weary se'nnights nine times nine
 Shall he dwindle, peak, and pine:
 Though his bark cannot be lost,   25
 Yet it shall be tempest-toss'd.
 Look what I have.
Second Witch: Show me, show me.

33   *weird:* comes from the Saxon word *wyrd* meaning fate. Thus the witches are describing themselves as foretellers of fate or destiny.

34   *posters:* swift travellers

45   *choppy:* chapped. The witches indicate that they will not reply to Banquo, or perhaps that they will not reply to any questions from a human.

47   *beards:* It was common belief that witches were bearded.

50   *Glamis:* the traditional domain of the Macbeth family. Macbeth would have inherited the title of Thane of Glamis from his father. Their castle may still be seen in Scotland today.

54-55   *seem to fear/Things which do sound so fair:* a pun

56   *fantastical:* creatures of the imagination

60   *rapt:* dazed

First Witch: Here I have a pilot's thumb,
    Wreck'd, as homeward he did come.   [*Drum within*] 30
Third Witch: A drum, a drum!
    Macbeth doth come.
All: The weird sisters, hand in hand,
    Posters of the sea and land,
    Thus do go about, about; 35
    Thrice to thine, and thrice to mine,
    And thrice again, to make up nine.
    Peace! the charm's wound up.
    [*Enter Macbeth and Banquo*]
Macbeth: So foul and fair a day I have not seen.
Banquo: How far is't call'd to Forres? What are these 40
    So wither'd, and so wild in their attire,
    That look not like the inhabitants o' the earth,
    And yet are on't? Live you? or are you aught
    That man may question? You seem to understand me,
    By each at once her choppy finger laying 45
    Upon her skinny lips: you should be women,
    And yet your beards forbid me to interpret
    That you are so.
Macbeth: Speak, if you can: what are you?
First Witch: All hail, Macbeth! hail to thee, thane of Glamis! 50
Second Witch: All hail, Macbeth! hail to thee, thane of
    Cawdor!
Third Witch: All hail, Macbeth! that shalt be king hereafter.
Banquo: Good sir, why do you start, and seem to fear
    Things that do sound so fair? I' the name of truth, 55
    Are ye fantastical, or that indeed
    Which outwardly ye show? My noble partner
    You greet with present grace and great prediction
    Of noble having, and of royal hope,
    That he seems rapt withal; to me you speak not: 60
    If you can look into the seeds of time,
    And say which grain will grow and which will not,
    Speak then to me, who neither beg nor fear
    Your favours nor your hate.
First Witch: Hail! 65
Second Witch: Hail!
Third Witch: Hail!

70   *get:* beget, be the father of

73   *imperfect:* they have not stated all that he wants to know

74   *Sinel:* Macbeth's father

75   *the Thane of Cawdor lives:* Macbeth evidently does not know
       of Cawdor's treachery, despite his own role in the traitor's defeat.

79   *owe:* have received, possess

84   *corporal:* physical, tangible

87   *the insane root:* a root which makes the eater insane. It was
       believed that this was a property of poisonous plants such as
       hemlock, deadly nightshade, and henbane.

96-97 *His wonders and his praises do contend . . . silenced with that:*
       Duncan's response to Macbeth's actions alternates between
       astonishment and gratitude. He is overwhelmed and left
       speechless by Macbeth's bravery.

100-101 *Nothing afeard . . . images of death:* Although Macbeth was killing
       so many of the enemy, he clearly did not fear death himself.

102   *post with post:* messenger after messenger

First Witch: Lesser than Macbeth, and greater.
Second Witch: Not so happy, yet much happier.
Third Witch: Thou shalt get kings, though thou be none: 70
    So all hail, Macbeth and Banquo!
First Witch: Banquo, and Macbeth, all hail!
Macbeth: Stay, you imperfect speakers, tell me more:
    By Sinel's death I know I am thane of Glamis;
    But how of Cawdor? the thane of Cawdor lives,   75
    A prosperous gentleman; and to be king
    Stands not within the prospect of belief,
    No more than to be Cawdor. Say from whence
    You owe this strange intelligence? or why
    Upon this blasted heath you stop our way   80
    With such prophetic greeting? Speak, I charge you.
                             [Witches vanish]
Banquo: The earth hath bubbles, as the water has,
    And these are of them: whither are they vanish'd?
Macbeth: Into the air: and what seem'd corporal melted
    As breath into the wind. 'Would they had stay'd!   85
Banquo: Were such things here as we do speak about?
    Or have we eaten on the insane root
    That takes the reason prisoner?
Macbeth: Your children shall be kings.
Banquo: You shall be king.   90
Macbeth: And thane of Cawdor too; went it not so?
Banquo: To the self-same tune and words. Who's here?
    [Enter Ross and Angus]
Ross: The king hath happily received, Macbeth,
    The news of thy success: and when he reads
    Thy personal venture in the rebels' fight,   95
    His wonders and his praises do contend
    Which should be thine, or his: silenced with that,
    In viewing o'er the rest o' the self-same day,
    He finds thee in the stout Norweyan ranks,
    Nothing afeard of what thyself didst make,   100
    Strange images of death. As thick as hail
    Came post with post; and every one did bear
    Thy praises in his kingdom's great defence,
    And pour'd them down before him.
Angus: We are sent,   105

109   *for an earnest:* as a pledge, promise

111   *addition:* new title

119-120 *or did line the rebel/With hidden help and vantage:* Cawdor may have given secret help to the rebel Macdonwald.

125   *behind:* still to come

129   *trusted home:* taken to its conclusion

135   *in deepest consequence:* in matters that are of great significance

137-139 *Two truths are told . . . the imperial theme:* The theatre metaphor indicates that Macbeth sees the apparent accuracy of the first two predictions as a prologue which will lead to the play's major action: the kingship.

144   *that suggestion:* Macbeth has a mental image of himself killing Duncan.

To give thee, from our royal master, thanks;
Only to herald thee into his sight,
Not pay thee.
Ross: And, for an earnest of a greater honour,
He bade me, from him, call thee thane of Cawdor: 110
In which addition, hail, most worthy thane!
For it is thine.
Banquo: What, can the devil speak true?
Macbeth: The thane of Cawdor lives: why do you dress me
In borrow'd robes?   115
Angus: Who was the thane lives yet;
But under heavy judgment bears that life
Which he deserves to lose. Whether he was combined
With those of Norway, or did line the rebel
With hidden help and vantage; or that with both   120
He labour'd in his country's wreck, I know not;
But treasons capital, confess'd, and proved,
Have overthrown him.
Macbeth [Aside]:   Glamis, and thane of Cawdor:
The greatest is behind.—Thanks for your pains.—   125
Do you not hope your children shall be kings,
When those that gave the thane of Cawdor to me,
Promised no less to them?
Banquo: That, trusted home,
Might yet enkindle you unto the crown,   130
Besides the thane of Cawdor. But 'tis strange:
And oftentimes, to win us to our harm,
The instruments of darkness tell us truths,
Win us with honest trifles, to betray us
In deepest consequence.   135
Cousins, a word, I pray you.
Macbeth [Aside]:   Two truths are told,
As happy prologues to the swelling act
Of the imperial theme.—I thank you, gentlemen.—
[*Aside*] This supernatural soliciting   140
Cannot be ill; cannot be good: if ill,
Why hath it given me earnest of success,
Commencing in a truth? I am thane of Cawdor:
If good, why do I yield to that suggestion
Whose horrid image doth unfix my hair   145

147-148   *Present fears/Are less than horrible imaginings:* A vivid imagination is more frightening than reality.

150   *single state of man:* the harmony of the body and mind working together; *function:* reality

151   *surmise:* conjecture, imagination

153   *rapt:* preoccupied, dreaming

154   *chance:* fortune, destiny

156   *without my stir:* even if I do not take direct action

158   *strange garments . . . use:* New clothing does not fit well until we have worn it for a while.

160-161   *Come what, come may . . . roughest day:* The modern equivalent is, Whatever will be, will be.

162   *we stay upon your leisure:* We are waiting for you.

163   *my dull brain was wrought/With things forgotten:* I was trying to recall some past events.

164-166   *Your pains/Are registered . . . to read them:* Your kindness is recorded in my memory. Macbeth's metaphor is from journal-keeping or reading.

168   *the interim . . . it:* when we have had enough time to think about these events

169   *free hearts:* true feelings

And make my seated heart knock at my ribs,
Against the use of nature? Present fears
Are less than horrible imaginings:
My thought, whose murder yet is but fantastical,
Shakes so my single state of man that function   150
Is smother'd in surmise; and nothing is
But what is not.
Banquo: Look, how our partner's rapt.
Macbeth [Aside]: If chance will have me king, why, chance
    may crown me,   155
Without my stir.
Banquo: New honours come upon him,
Like our strange garments, cleave not to their mould,
But with the aid of use.
Macbeth [Aside]:   Come what come may,   160
Time and the hour runs through the roughest day.
Banquo: Worthy Macbeth, we stay upon your leisure.
Macbeth: Give me your favour: my dull brain was wrought
With things forgotten. Kind gentlemen, your pains
Are register'd where every day I turn   165
The leaf to read them. Let us toward the king.
Think upon what hath chanced, and at more time,
The interim having weigh'd it, let us speak
Our free hearts each to other.
Banquo: Very gladly.   170
Macbeth: Till then, enough. Come, friends.

                              [*Exeunt*]

Act 1, Scene 3: Activities

1. As a director, how would you costume and present the witches? Outline your ideas in a director's log.

2. With a partner, choose a piece of music that might provide an appropriate theme for the witches' scenes. Play your choice to your group and judge its effectiveness by the group's descriptions of what the music suggests.

3. Assume that the actors who play the witches have complained to Shakespeare that the first 30 lines of this scene make the witches seem silly rather than evil. Prepare Shakespeare's response, defending the opening.

4. Record in a personal journal entry whether you would have preferred to receive the prophecies made to Macbeth or those made to Banquo.

5. Based on what you see of Macbeth in this scene, do you admire him? How does your reaction compare with your response to the reports of him in the previous scene? Share your ideas with others.

6. Script a brief dialogue Ross and Angus might have when they arrive at Forres later that night, recalling the events of the day and predicting the consequences.

7. If you had advice to give Macbeth, what would it be? Do you think he would take your advice? Role-play the conversation for an audience.

For the next scene . . .

In your journal describe an experience in which you misjudged someone or were misled by someone's attractiveness.

Act 1, Scene 4

In this scene . . .

The scene opens as Malcolm is describing to Duncan the execution of the former Thane of Cawdor. Just as the king is admitting that he was badly misled by the traitor's appearance, he is interrupted by the entrance of Macbeth who is accompanied by Banquo, Ross, and Angus. The king thanks his generals, and promises to reward them with more honours. He then formally names his son Malcolm as his successor. As a sign of honour to Macbeth, Duncan invites himself and the court to visit Macbeth's castle at Inverness. Macbeth replies with compliments and leaves immediately to prepare his castle for the king's visit, but he is shaken by the king's unprecedented naming of his heir.

2   *Those in commission:* those charged with the responsibility

3   *liege:* lord

7   *set forth:* showed

9   *became him:* suited him

10   *that had been studied:* like an actor, had learned and rehearsed
     his lines well

11   *owed:* owned

13-14 *There's no art . . . in the face:* It is impossible to learn how to
       judge a person's character by appearance.

19-21 *thou art so far before . . . To overtake thee:* You deserve more
       thanks than it is possible to give. The metaphor is based on
       a swiftly flying bird overtaking its quarry.

21-23 *Would thou hadst less deserved . . . have been mine:* If Macbeth
       had deserved less, Duncan might have been able to thank and
       repay him more appropriately.

24   *More is thy due . . . all can pay:* I owe you more than I can ever
     repay.

26   *pays itself:* is a reward in itself

Scene 4

Forres. A room in the Palace.

Flourish. Enter Duncan, Malcolm,
Donalbain, Lennox and
Attendants.

Duncan: Is execution done on Cawdor? Are not
  Those in commission yet return'd?
Malcolm: My liege,
  They are not yet come back. But I have spoke
  With one that saw him die, who did report   5
  That very frankly he confess'd his treasons,
  Implored your highness' pardon, and set forth
  A deep repentance: nothing in his life
  Became him like the leaving it; he died
  As one that had been studied in his death,   10
  To throw away the dearest thing he owed,
  As 'twere a careless trifle.
Duncan: There's no art
  To find the mind's construction in the face:
  He was a gentleman on whom I built,   15
  An absolute trust.
          [*Enter Macbeth, Banquo, Ross and Angus*]
                    O worthiest cousin!
  The sin of my ingratitude even now
  Was heavy on me: thou art so far before,
  That swiftest wing of recompense is slow   20
  To overtake thee. Would thou hadst less deserved;
  That the proportion both of thanks and payment
  Might have been mine! only I have left to say,
  More is thy due than more than all can pay.
Macbeth: The service and the loyalty I owe,   25
  In doing it, pays itself. Your highness' part
  Is to receive our duties: and our duties
  Are to your throne and state, children and servants;

29 *everything/Safe toward your love and honour:* everything possible to safeguard your honour and security.

32-33 *I have begun to plant thee . . . full of growing:* Duncan suggests that he will look for more ways to honour Macbeth. The metaphor Duncan uses has fertility as the object of comparison.

39-41 *My plenteous joys . . . drops of sorrow:* Duncan cannot control his tears of joy.

43 *establish our estate:* name my successor. The Prince of Cumberland was the title given to the heir to the throne.

47 *signs of nobleness . . . shall shine:* symbols of nobility will be awarded.

48 *Inverness:* Macbeth's castle (see map, page 4)

49 *bind:* increase our debt

50 *The rest is labour:* I prefer to spend time in your service rather than in relaxation.

51 *harbinger:* an officer of the king's household who goes ahead to prepare for the king's reception and accommodation

55 *a step:* an obstacle

58 *Let not light . . . desires:* Macbeth calls on darkness to hide his evil thoughts.

59 *The eye wink at the hand:* Let the eye be blind to what the hand is doing.

59-60 *yet let that be . . . to see:* Macbeth asks the stars to make his desire a reality despite his horror at the action he is planning to take.

61-63 *he is full so valiant . . . banquet to me:* Duncan is continuing a conversation with Banquo in which they have been praising Macbeth.

64 *whose care . . . welcome:* whose concern has prompted him to go ahead to make preparations

Which do but what they should, by doing everything
Safe toward your love and honour. 30
Duncan: Welcome hither:
I have begun to plant thee, and will labour
To make thee full of growing. Noble Banquo,
That hast no less deserved, nor must be known
No less to have done so: let me enfold thee 35
And hold thee to my heart.
Banquo: There if I grow,
The harvest is your own.
Duncan: My plenteous joys,
Wanton in fulness, seek to hide themselves 40
In drops of sorrow. Sons, kinsmen, thanes,
And you whose places are the nearest, know,
We will establish our estate upon
Our eldest, Malcolm, whom we name hereafter
The Prince of Cumberland: which honour must 45
Not, unaccompanied, invest him only,
But signs of nobleness, like stars, shall shine
On all deservers. From hence to Inverness,
And bind us further to you.
Macbeth: The rest is labour, which is not used for you; 50
I'll be myself the harbinger, and make joyful
The hearing of my wife with your approach;
So humbly take my leave.
Duncan: My worthy Cawdor!
Macbeth: [*Aside*] The Prince of Cumberland! that is a step 55
On which I must fall down, or else o'er-leap,
For in my way it lies. Stars, hide your fires;
Let not light see my black and deep desires:
The eye wink at the hand! yet let that be,
Which the eye fears, when it is done, to see [*Exit*] 60
Duncan: True, worthy Banquo; he is full so valiant,
And in his commendations I am fed;
It is a banquet to me. Let's after him,
Whose care is gone before to bid us welcome:
It is a peerless kinsman. [*Flourish. Exeunt*]

Act 1, Scene 4: Activities

1. The Thane of Cawdor accepts his execution stoically. Do you think such a self-controlled acceptance of one's death is seen as admirable today? Explain your response.

2. Writers use irony frequently to present life's unpredictability and complexity. What are some examples of irony that you have experienced or heard about? Share them with a partner. Then identify and explain some examples of irony in this scene.

3. In your groups, read aloud lines 17–49 in which Duncan thanks his generals and they respond. What differences do you notice between Macbeth's and Banquo's replies to Duncan? What do you conclude from these differences?

4. As the court reporter for one of Scotland's largest newspapers, you have some important events to report. Write the news story, keeping in mind the following:
   • A well-known Scotsman has been executed.
   • His title has been given to someone else.
   • The king is holding his first court since his recent victory.
   • The king has taken the unprecedented step of naming his son as his successor. (In medieval Scotland the king's son did not have hereditary rights.)
   • The court is about to embark on a journey.

For the next scene . . .

In your journal, write about a time when you persuaded someone to do something, or a situation in which you were persuaded to do something about which you felt hesitant. Describe the consequences and feelings that resulted.

Act 1, Scene 5

In this scene . . .

At the Macbeths' castle in Inverness, Lady Macbeth is reading a letter her husband has sent to tell her of the prophecies and their partial fulfilment. Lady Macbeth expresses her determination that the third prophecy will also come true. Nevertheless, she believes that Macbeth is not capable of the direct action required – that is, the murder of Duncan – and determines to spur him on. A messenger arrives with the news that Duncan is on his way to Inverness. Realizing that Duncan's visit will be an ideal opportunity to carry out her plan, she calls on the spirits of darkness and evil to replace all her nurturing, feminine qualities with remorseless cruelty. Macbeth arrives and is assured by Lady Macbeth that she will manage the clearly understood, but unstated scheme they have in mind. She reminds him that he should appear to be welcoming and loyal, to hide their real intentions.

2   *perfectest report:* Macbeth may mean the fulfilment of the pre-dictions that he would be both Thane of Glamis and Thane of Cawdor.

3   *mortal:* human

6   *missives:* messengers

9   *the coming on of time:* the future

10   *deliver:* communicate, report

11-12   *that thou mightest not lose the/dues of rejoicing:* so that you will not be denied your share of the rejoicing

16   *the milk of human kindness:* gentleness or, perhaps, common humanity or decency

17   *the nearest way:* the most direct path; in this case, murder

19   *The illness should attend it:* the wickedness that should accom-pany ambition

19-20   *what thou wouldst highly . . . holily:* When you want something passionately, you also want to obtain it by fair means.

20-21   *wouldst not play false . . . win:* You would not act dishonestly, yet you would be happy to enjoy ill-gotten gains. The metaphor is based on gambling.

21-24   *thou'dst have, great Glamis . . . should be undone:* You would rather have the crown by doing what you fear to do (the murder) than not have it, despite the actions necessary to obtain it.

24   *Hie thee hither:* Hurry home.

26   *chastise with the valour of my tongue:* drive away with fearless words

27   *impedes:* stands in your way; *golden round:* crown

Scene 5

*Inverness. A room in Macbeth's
Castle.*

*Enter Lady Macbeth, reading a
letter.*

Lady Macbeth: 'They met me in the day of success; and I
have learned by the perfectest report, they have more in
them than mortal knowledge. When I burned in desire
to question them further, they made themselves air, into
which they vanished. Whiles I stood rapt in the   5
wonder of it, came missives from the king, who all-
hailed me, "Thane of Cawdor"; by which title, before,
these weird sisters saluted me, and referred me to the
coming on of time, with "Hail, king that shalt be!"
This have I thought good to deliver thee, my dearest   10
partner of greatness; that thou mightest not lose the
dues of rejoicing, by being ignorant of what greatness
is promised thee. Lay it to thy heart, and farewell.'

Glamis thou art, and Cawdor, and shalt be
What thou art promised: yet do I fear thy nature;   15
It is too full o' the milk of human kindness
To catch the nearest way: thou wouldst be great:
Art not without ambition, but without
The illness should attend it; what thou wouldst highly,
That wouldst thou holily; wouldst not play false,   20
And yet wouldst wrongly win: thou'dst have, great Glamis,
That which cries, "Thus must thou do, if thou have it,"
And that which rather thou dost fear to do
Than wishest should be undone. Hie thee hither,
That I may pour my spirits in thine ear,   25
And chastise with the valour of my tongue
All that impedes thee from the golden round,

28   *metaphysical:* supernatural

29   *withal:* with

32-34 *Thou'rt mad to say it . . . for preparation:* Being unprepared for this news, Lady Macbeth may think the messenger means Macbeth, or perhaps she is amazed at how well Duncan's arrival will suit her plans. She then tries to justify her amazement to the servant.

36   *speed of him:* overtook the messenger

41   *The raven:* Ravens were believed to be messengers of evil tidings.

44   *tend on mortal thoughts:* take care of, look after thoughts of murder; *unsex:* take away all feminine qualities

47   *stop:* block

48   *compunctious visitings:* compassionate, natural feelings

49   *fell:* savage

49-50 *nor keep peace . . . effect and it:* so that no peacemaker intervenes between the purpose and the deed

51   *take my milk for gall:* replace nourishing milk with bile, a bitter substance found in the gall-bladder.

51   *you murdering ministers:* the agents of evil

52   *sightless substances:* invisible forms

53   *You wait on nature's mischief:* You are ready to assist in upsetting natural harmony; that is, in carrying out evil.

54   *pall thee in the dunnest smoke:* wrap yourself (as in a pall) in the darkest smoke

57   *Hold, hold!:* Stop!

59   *all-hail hereafter:* a reference to the third prophecy, that Macbeth would become king in the future

61   *ignorant present:* the present does not know of the future

61-62 *I feel now the future in the instant:* Her thoughts makes the future a reality now.

Which fate and metaphysical aid doth seem
To have thee crown'd withal.
[*Enter a Messenger*]
                          What is your tidings?   30
Messenger: The king comes here to-night.
Lady Macbeth: Thou'rt mad to say it:
  Is not thy master with him? who, were't so,
  Would have inform'd for preparation.
Messenger: So please you, it is true; our thane is coming: 35
  One of my fellows had the speed of him,
  Who, almost dead for breath, had scarcely more
  Than would make up his message.
Lady Macbeth: Give him tending;
  He brings great news.   [*Exit Messenger*]   40
                 The raven himself is hoarse
  That croaks the fatal entrance of Duncan
  Under my battlements. Come, you spirits
  That tend on mortal thoughts, unsex me here,
  And fill me, from the crown to the toe, top-full   45
  Of direst cruelty! make thick my blood,
  Stop up the access and passage to remorse,
  That no compunctious visitings of nature
  Shake my fell purpose, nor keep peace between
  The effect and it! Come to my woman's breasts,   50
  And take my milk for gall, you murdering ministers,
  Wherever in your sightless substances
  You wait on nature's mischief! Come, thick night,
  And pall thee in the dunnest smoke of hell,
  That my keen knife see not the wound it makes,   55
  Nor heaven peep through the blanket of the dark,
  To cry, "Hold, hold!"
[*Enter Macbeth*]
                 Great Glamis, worthy Cawdor!
  Greater than both, by the all-hail hereafter!
  Thy letters have transported me beyond   60
  This ignorant present, and I feel now
  The future in the instant.
Macbeth: My dearest love,
  Duncan comes here to-night.
Lady Macbeth: And when goes hence?   65

70-71   *To beguile the time,/Look like the time:* In order to deceive the world, look as people expect you to look. In this case, Macbeth should seem to be the hospitable and honoured host of the king.

73-74   *He that's coming/Must be provided for:* Appropriate preparations must be made.

75   *my dispatch:* management

77   *solely sovereign sway:* absolute royal power to us

79   *look up clear:* raise your eyes, look confident

80   *favour:* face; *To alter favour ever is to fear:* A change in the way one looks reveals fear (and thus arouses suspicion).

Macbeth: To-morrow, as he purposes.
Lady Macbeth: O, never
   Shall sun that morrow see!
   Your face, my thane, is as a book, where men
   May read strange matters. To beguile the time,   70
   Look like the time; bear welcome in your eye,
   Your hand, your tongue: look like the innocent flower,
   But be the serpent under it. He that's coming
   Must be provided for: and you shall put
   This night's great business into my dispatch;   75
   Which shall to all our nights and days to come
   Give solely sovereign sway and masterdom.
Macbeth: We will speak further.
Lady Macbeth: Only look up clear;
   To alter favour ever is to fear: 80
   Leave all the rest to me.

                                     [Exeunt]

Act 1, Scene 5: Activities

1. In your group, rehearse Lady Macbeth's lines 14–29 and 39–62. Choose one member to present the readings to the class. Compare the interpretations of different readers, discussing the effect and validity of each one.

2. Make a list of all of the Macbeths' characteristics you know about at this point in the play. Add to the list as you continue through the play.

3. How do you go about achieving a goal that is very important to you? What main sources of assistance do you depend on? What does Lady Macbeth depend on to give her assistance.

4. In your journal, describe the Macbeth's marriage. Assess whether it conforms to your idea of a good marriage.

5. In a director's log, note how Macbeth should behave in this scene. Should his actions bear out Lady Macbeth's assessment that "thy nature, it is too full o' the milk of human kindness" (lines 15–16)?

For the next scene . . .

In your journal, record a situation in which you have been
hypocritical or insincere. Describe the circumstances. Were
you happy with the outcome? Would you behave the same
way again?

Act 1, Scene 6

In this scene . . .

In contrast to most scenes in the play, this one takes place in daylight and in a beautiful and serene setting. With the exception of Macbeth, all the play's major characters are present as Lady Macbeth greets the king and his court. Duncan is generous in his praise and compliments.

Stage direction—*Hautboys:* a musical instrument like an oboe. Shakespeare uses the word "hautboy" for both the instrument and its player.

1   *seat:* situation, location

1-3   *the air/Nimbly . . . our gentle senses:* The senses are soothed by the brisk, sweet air.

5   *martlet:* martin, a member of the swallow family

5-7   *The temple-haunting martlet . . . smells wooingly here:* The martin, which usually builds its nests near churches, proves the sweetness of the air here by choosing the castle for its home.

7   *jutty:* corner of house jutting out; *frieze:* a decorative band

8   *buttress:* supporting projection; *coign of vantage:* convenient corner

9   *pendent bed:* hanging nest; *procreant cradle:* the nest for the young

10   *haunt:* frequent, visit

13-16   *The love that follows us . . . for your trouble:* Even though the love of my subjects is sometimes an inconvenience, I am still grateful for it. I, too, am causing inconvenience, but by doing so I am teaching you to thank me for my love, for love is the reason for my visit.

19   *single business:* feeble service, poor by comparison with the king's rewards

23   *We rest your hermits:* We are bound to pray for you.

25   *coursed:* followed

Scene 6

The Same. Before the Castle.
Hautboys. Servants of Macbeth
attending.

Enter Duncan, Malcolm,
Donalbain, Banquo, Lennox,
Macduff, Ross, Angus and
Attendants.

Duncan: This castle hath a pleasant seat; the air
  Nimbly and sweetly recommends itself
  Unto our gentle senses.
Banquo: This guest of summer,
  The temple-haunting martlet, does approve,   5
  By his loved mansionry, that the heaven's breath
  Smells wooingly here: no jutty, frieze,
  Buttress, nor coign of vantage, but this bird
  Hath made his pendent bed and procreant cradle:
  Where they most breed and haunt, I have observed,   10
  The air is delicate.
  [Enter Lady Macbeth]
Duncan: See, see! our honour'd hostess!
  The love that follows us sometime is our trouble,
  Which still we thank as love. Herein I teach you,
  How you shall bid God 'ild us for your pains,   15
  And thank us for your trouble.
Lady Macbeth: All our service
  In every point twice done, and then done double,
  Were poor and single business, to contend
  Against those honours deep and broad, wherewith   20
  Your majesty loads our house: for those of old,
  And the late dignities heap'd up to them,
  We rest your hermits.
Duncan: Where's the thane of Cawdor?
  We coursed him at the heels, and had a purpose   25

26   *purveyor:* someone who rides ahead of the king, to ensure that food is ready for the royal party

27   *holp:* helped

30-33   *Your servants ever . . . return your own:* The Macbeths are the king's subjects. Everything they own is, in fact, the property of the king. They hold it all in trust *(compt)* for the king, ready to give him an account *(to make their audit)* whenever he wishes, and to return to him always *(still)* what he owns.

37   *By your leave, hostess:* The king may kiss her cheek or take her hand.

To be his purveyor: but he rides well,
And his great love, sharp as his spur, hath holp him
To his home before us. Fair and noble hostess,
We are your guest to-night.

Lady Macbeth: Your servants ever   30
Have theirs, themselves, and what is theirs, in compt,
To make their audit at your highness' pleasure,
Still to return your own.

Duncan: Give me your hand:
Conduct me to mine host; we love him highly,   35
And shall continue our graces towards him.
By your leave, hostess.   [*Exeunt*]

Act 1, Scene 6: Activities

1. Reduce Lady Macbeth's lines in this scene to their literal meaning. After reading your new speech to your group, compare the effect of your version with the effect of Lady Macbeth's original lines.

2. Although Macbeth chooses not to greet his royal guest, imagine that he is observing Duncan's arrival at Inverness, perhaps from a window or a battlement. Write a short soliloquy in which he explains why he chose not to meet the king. You could give a dramatic reading of your soliloquy to the class.

3. How would you illustrate this scene? After you have sketched or described your illustration, examine the illustration on page 46. Discuss with your group how it matches or departs from your mental image.

For the next scene . . .

Recall a time when you wanted something so badly that nothing else mattered but achieving your desire. Did you succeed or did you fail? How did you feel about what happened?

Act 1, Scene 7

In this scene . . .

Macbeth leaves the grand banquet that he is holding in honour of Duncan. He needs time and privacy to consider his terrible conflict: he wants the throne but is appalled at the thought of killing his king. He thinks of a number of reasons for not going any further with his plans when Lady Macbeth, feeling uneasy at his absence, interrupts him. Macbeth tells her that he has decided not to murder Duncan. Scornfully, she accuses him of inconstancy, cowardice, and unmanliness. She emphasises her own strength by declaring that she would rather kill her child than withdraw from a solemn commitment. Macbeth finally agrees to proceed when Lady Macbeth presents her plan: she will ply Duncan's attendants with so much liquor that they will be oblivious, and then she and her husband will stab the king with his servants' weapons.

Stage direction—*Sewer:* the chief servant or butler, who was responsible for the arranging of the banquet. Originally, he was the official taster, ensuring that the king's food was not poisoned; *divers:* several, various; *service:* utensils

1-2	*If it were done . . . done quickly:* If the murder were finished with once it had been committed, it would be best to commit it soon.
3	*trammel:* to catch in a net, that is, prevent
4	*surcease:* death; *that but:* so that only
6	*upon this bank and shoal of time:* at this particular moment in time. The metaphor presents the moment as a sandbank in the sea of eternity.
7	*jump the life to come:* risk the consequences we might have to face in an after-life
8	*still have judgment here:* We always have judgment in this life.
8-10	*that we but teach . . . inventor:* Even if we do no worse than teach others to be evil, evil will return to torment the original teacher.
10	*even-handed justice:* Justice is fair; that is, justice offers back to us the same ingredients that we used to commit a crime.
11	*Commends:* presents, offers; *chalice:* cup; the sacred goblet of holy communion
17	*borne his faculties so meek:* has used his powers so humbly, or with such moderation
18	*clear:* faultless, honest
20	*taking-off:* murder
21-25	*and pity . . . drown the wind:* Macbeth personifies pity as a baby (a symbol of helplessness) or an angel (a symbol of innocence) riding on the winds and blowing the news of the murder into everyone's eyes. Just as dust blowing into one's eyes causes tears, so news of the murder will cause weeping. As rain follows from wind, so tears of sorrow will follow from pity for Duncan.
23	*sightless:* invisible
25-28	*I have no spur . . . falls on the other:* Macbeth admits that it is only ambition that spurs him on. Using images of horseriding, he compares this ambition to an over-eager rider who, in trying to leap onto his horse's saddle, leaps over the horse.

Scene 7

The same. A room in the Castle.

Hautboys and torches. Enter, and pass over the Stage, a Sewer, and divers Servants with dishes and service.

Then enter Macbeth.

Macbeth: If it were done, when 'tis done, then 'twere well
It were done quickly: if the assassination
Could trammel up the consequence, and catch,
With his surcease, success; that but this blow
Might be the be-all and the end-all here,   5
But here, upon this bank and shoal of time,
We'd jump the life to come. But in these cases,
We still have judgment here; that we but teach
Bloody instructions, which being taught return
To plague the inventor: this even-handed justice   10
Commends the ingredients of our poison'd chalice
To our own lips. He's here in double trust:
First, as I am his kinsman and his subject,
Strong both against the deed: then, as his host,
Who should against his murderer shut the door,   15
Not bear the knife myself. Besides, this Duncan
Hath borne his faculties so meek, hath been
So clear in his great office, that his virtues
Will plead like angels, trumpet-tongued, against
The deep damnation of his taking off;   20
And pity, like a naked new-born babe,
Striding the blast, or heaven's cherubin horsed
Upon the sightless couriers of the air,
Shall blow the horrid deed in every eye,
That tears shall drown the wind. I have no spur   25
To prick the sides of my intent, but only

34	*bought:* earned
36	*would:* should
36	*be worn now in their newest gloss:* Macbeth compares the enjoyment of praise and honour with the wearing of new clothes.
38	*hope:* Macbeth's desire to be king
40	*so green and pale:* Macbeth's original hope must have a hangover.
42	*such I account thy love:* Your love can be no more dependable and lasting than your earlier desire.
45	*esteems't:* value as; *the ornament of life:* the crown
46	*esteem:* respect
47	*wait upon:* be subservient to
48	*adage:* proverb. "The cat would eat fish but would not wet her feet."
49	*prithee:* I pray you, please.
50	*become:* be right for
51	*Who dares do more is none:* Anyone who would do more would become less than a man; that is he would lose his humanity.
54	*durst:* dared
57	*did then adhere:* were at that time in your favour
57	*yet you would make both:* you considered making the opportunity
58-59	*They have made themselves . . . unmake you:* Now that the opportunity has presented itself, it makes you fearful.
59	*I have given suck:* I have nursed a baby.

Vaulting ambition, which o'erleaps itself
And falls on the other.
[*Enter Lady Macbeth*]
Lady Macbeth: How now, what news?
   He has almost supp'd: why have you left the chamber!   30
Macbeth: Hath he ask'd for me?
Lady Macbeth: Know you not he has?
Macbeth: We will proceed no further in this business:
   He hath honour'd me of late; and I have bought
   Golden opinions from all sorts of people,   35
   Which would be worn now in their newest gloss,
   Not cast aside so soon.
Lady Macbeth: Was the hope drunk
   Wherein you dress'd yourself? hath it slept since?
   And wakes it now, to look so green and pale   40
   At what it did so freely? From this time
   Such I account thy love. Art thou afeard
   To be the same in thine own act and valour
   As thou art in desire? Wouldst thou have that
   Which thou esteem'st the ornament of life,   45
   And live a coward in thine own esteem,
   Letting "I dare not" wait upon "I would,"
   Like the poor cat i' the adage?
Macbeth: Prithee, peace:
   I dare do all that may become a man;   50
   Who dares do more, is none.
Lady Macbeth: What beast was't then
   That made you break this enterprise to me?
   When you durst do it, then you were a man;
   And, to be more than what you were, you would   55
   Be so much more the man. Nor time nor place
   Did then adhere, and yet you would make both:
   They have made themselves, and that their fitness now
   Does unmake you. I have given suck, and know
   How tender 'tis to love the babe that milks me: 60
   I would, while it was smiling in my face,
   Have pluck'd my nipple from his boneless gums,
   And dash'd the brains out, had I so sworn
   As you have done to this.
Macbeth: If we should fail?   65

67   *screw your courage to the sticking place:* The metaphor refers to the tuning of a stringed musical instrument such as a lute, guitar, or violin, or to the tightening of the string of a cross-bow. In either case, when the string is taut, it has reached its "sticking place".

71   *wassel:* revelry, merrymaking; *convince:* overpower, overcome

74   *limbeck:* a still, filled with alcohol. It was believed that memory, located at the base of the brain, guarded against vapours rising from the body. Body vapours would affect the ability of the brain to reason. Drinking alcohol converted memory to a fume or vapour, so the brain lost its protection and its capacity to function properly.

75   *drenched:* drowned

78   *spongy:* drunken

79   *quell:* murder

81   *mettle:* metal, that is, material or substance

82   *received:* thought, believed

86   *other:* in any other way

87   *As:* seeing how

89-90   *bend up/Each corporal agent:* Macbeth suggests he will strain every part of his body. His metaphor is based on stringing a bow.

91   *mock the time:* deceive all observers

Lady Macbeth: We fail!
But screw your courage to the sticking place,
And we'll not fail. When Duncan is asleep—
Whereto the rather shall his day's hard journey
Soundly invite him—his two chamberlains   70
Will I with wine and wassel so convince,
That memory, the warder of the brain,
Shall be a fume, and the receipt of reason
A limbeck only: when in swinish sleep
Their drenched natures lie as in a death,   75
What cannot you and I perform upon
The unguarded Duncan? what not put upon
His spongy officers who shall bear the guilt
Of our great quell?
Macbeth: Bring forth men-children only,   80
For thy undaunted mettle should compose
Nothing but males. Will it not be received,
When we have mark'd with blood those sleepy two
Of his own chamber, and used their very daggers,
That they have done't?   85
Lady Macbeth: Who dares receive it other,
As we shall make our griefs and clamour roar
Upon his death?
Macbeth: I am settled, and bend up
Each corporal agent to this terrible feat.   90
Away, and mock the time with fairest show:
False face must hide what the false heart doth know.
                                        [*Exeunt*]

Act 1, Scene 7: Activities

1. Choose one of the following topics and decide how Macbeth would feel about it. Share your ideas with your group. Learn what ideas other groups have about the topics you did not choose.

   - judgment after death; judgment during this life
   - duties of a subject; duties of a relative; duties of a host
   - Duncan's virtues; public outcry
   - motivation; consequences

2. Reread or listen to a recording of Macbeth's soliloquy at the beginning of the scene. How does this soliloquy add to your understanding of Macbeth or alter your opinion of him? Share your ideas with others.

3. Directors and actresses have always disagreed about how Lady Macbeth should deliver the line, "We fail." In your group, try as many ways as you can (for example, We fail? We fail. We fail!), and decide which is most satisfactory. Describe what kind of woman your interpretation suggests and compare your conclusions with those of other groups. Then write a character summary of Lady Macbeth based on your impressions of her.

4. Script the whispered conversation two of the Macbeths' servants might have as they observe, but do not overhear, this scene.

5. Discuss with your group the various techniques used by Lady Macbeth to convince her husband to murder Duncan. Decide which one is the most successful. Compare your decision with those of the rest of the class.

6. If Lady Macbeth asked for your reaction to her murder plan, how would you respond? Consider the arguments outlined by Macbeth in lines 1–28.

7. In your journal, a) define what you think "manliness" is; b) compare your definition with that of Lady Macbeth; c) record whether you think Macbeth meets your definition.

Act 1: Consider the Whole Act

1. Make a chart, listing on one side the factors that are tempting Macbeth to murder Duncan and, on the other, the factors that are holding him back. Predict the course of action he might take.

2. Imagine that, as Lady Macbeth's lady-in-waiting, you have observed changes in your mistress' behaviour. Write to a friend, describing your observations, expressing your curiosity about these changes, and speculating about causes and future behaviour.

3. Write Duncan's horoscope. Relate his character to events that you foresee happening.

4. With your group, list in separate columns the descriptions of Macbeth given by each of the following characters: the bleeding soldier, Duncan, the other thanes, Lady Macbeth, Macbeth himself. Underneath each column, note whether or not you agree with the description. Add a final column to list your own impressions of him.

5. Prepare three or four questions that you would like to ask Banquo. Ask a classmate to assume the character of Banquo, and interview him by asking your prepared questions. You could invite further questions from your audience.

6. How do you think the witches' words "Fair is foul, and foul is fair" apply to Act One? Write down your ideas and share them with a partner or your group. As you continue to study the play, see if you can find any more contradictions, describe them in your own words, and add them to your list.

7. Write the headline and opening sentences that a large sensation-oriented newspaper might publish after hearing a rumour that witches had recently been sighted. You could set this in Macbeth's time or today.

8. With the help of a librarian, research medieval and Renaissance beliefs about witchcraft. Consider the responses of Macbeth and Banquo to the witches. Decide whether their responses reflected or differed from your findings. Report your conclusions to your group.

9. Do some research into Scottish history, and prepare a report for class presentation. You might include information on how Macbeth and Duncan were related; on why Macbeth, historically, had a legitimate claim to the throne; on how the historical Macbeth and Duncan were killed; and on who became the successors to Macbeth.

For the next scene . . .

Most of us have been afraid of the dark at one time or another. Think of a time when you or someone you know felt frightened in the dark. Describe the experience in your journal, explaining how the person dealt with the terror.

Act 2, Scene 1

In this scene . . .

The night is dark and it is past midnight as Banquo and his son Fleance cross the palace courtyard on their way to bed. Banquo feels uneasy and is reluctant to sleep, for he fears that he will dream of the witches' prophecies. Macbeth enters and Banquo tells him of the king's pleasure in the hospitality at Inverness. The two agree to discuss the prophecies at some later time, although Banquo makes it clear that he will not talk about anything that is not loyal and honourable. When Macbeth is left alone, he yields to his vivid imagination: he sees a dagger in the air leading him towards the sleeping king and the deep silence of the night terrifies him. Suddenly a bell rings, a pre-arranged signal from Lady Macbeth that Duncan's servants are asleep and the time is right for Macbeth to enter Duncan's chamber.

1   *How goes the night?:* What time is it?

5   *husbandry:* thrift, economy

6   *their candles:* the stars; *take thee that too:* Having handed his sword to Fleance, Banquo then removes something else, perhaps his sword belt or his cloak.

7   *a heavy summons:* a strong desire to sleep

8   *Merciful powers:* Banquo is praying to the angels.

15   *largess:* gifts; *offices:* servants' quarters

16   *withal:* with

17   *shut up:* has gone to bed

19-21 *Being unprepared . . . free have wrought:* Because we were unprepared, we were unable to entertain the king as we would have wished.

26   *entreat an hour to serve:* agree on a convenient time

Act 2, Scene 1

Inverness. Court within the Castle.

*Enter Banquo and Fleance, and
a Servant with a torch before them.*

Banquo: How goes the night, boy?
Fleance: The moon is down; I have not heard the clock.
Banquo: And she goes down at twelve.
Fleance: I take't, 'tis later, sir.
Banquo: Hold, take my sword. There's husbandry in heaven,   5
   Their candles are all out. Take thee that too.
   A heavy summons lies like lead upon me,
   And yet I would not sleep. Merciful powers,
   Restrain in me the cursed thoughts that nature
   Gives way to in repose! Give me my sword.   10
   [*Enter Macbeth, and a Servant with a torch*]
   Who's there?
Macbeth: A friend.
Banquo: What, sir, not yet at rest? The king's a-bed:
   He hath been in unusual pleasure, and
   Sent forth great largess to your offices: 15
   This diamond he greets your wife withal,
   By the name of most kind hostess; and shut up
   In measureless content.
Macbeth: Being unprepared,
   Our will became the servant to defect,   20
   Which else should free have wrought.
Banquo: All's well.
   I dreamt last night of the three weird sisters:
   To you they have show'd some truth.
Macbeth: I think not of them: 25
   Yet, when we can entreat an hour to serve,

30   *If you shall cleave . . . when tis:* if you will support me when the time comes

32   *so:* provided that

33   *augment:* increase

34   *My bosom franchised and allegiance clear:* keep my conscience clear and remain loyal

43   *fatal:* prophetic, ominous; *sensible:* tangible

46   *heat-oppressed:* feverish

47   *palpable:* real, touchable

48   *this which now I draw:* Macbeth unsheaths his own dagger.

49   *Thou marshall'st me:* The dagger seems to move towards Duncan's room, directing Macbeth to follow.

51-52 *Mine eyes are made the fool . . . all the rest:* If the dagger is not real, then the other senses are correct and Macbeth's eyes are mistaken ("fools"); but if the dagger is real, then his eyes are more trustworthy than all the other senses.

53   *dudgeon:* handle; *gouts:* drops

55   *informs:* gives false information (literally, takes shape)

56   o'er the one half-world: our hemisphere is in darkness

57-58 *abuse/The curtain'd sleep:* tempt the sleeper. Macbeth imagines the sleeper in a four-poster bed with curtains drawn around it.

59   *Hecate:* the goddess of witches, sorcerers, and ghosts. She was also the goddess of roads and of the night. She haunted crossroads and graves, accompanied by terrifying hounds and the spirits of the dead.

59   *wither'd murder:* murder is personified as a ghost-like figure who stealthily moves towards his victim, as Tarquin did towards his. Tarquin (Tarquinius Sextus, the son of the last legendary king of Rome) raped Lucrece (the virtuous wife of a Roman officer) and this led to the expulsion of the Tarquin dynasty from Rome.

60   *Alarum'd:* aroused

61   thus: Macbeth imitates Tarquin's stealthy pace.

63   *sure:* immovable

We would spend it in some words upon that business,
If you would grant the time.
Banquo: At your kind'st leisure.
Macbeth: If you shall cleave to my consent, when 'tis   30
It shall make honour for you.
Banquo: So I lose none
In seeking to augment it, but still keep
My bosom franchised and allegiance clear,
I shall be counsell'd.   35
Macbeth: Good repose the while!
Banquo: Thanks, sir; the like to you!
                              [*Exit Banquo and Fleance*]
Macbeth: Go, bid thy mistress, when my drink is ready,
She strike upon the bell. Get thee to bed.
                                          [*Exit Servant*]
Is this a dagger which I see before me,   40
The handle toward my hand? Come, let me clutch thee.
I have thee not, and yet I see thee still.
Art thou not, fatal vision, sensible
To feeling as to sight? or art thou but
A dagger of the mind, a false creation,   45
Proceeding from the heat-oppressed brain?
I see thee yet, in form as palpable
As this which now I draw.
Thou marshall'st me the way that I was going;
And such an instrument I was to use.   50
Mine eyes are made the fools o' the other senses,
Or else worth all the rest: I see thee still;
And on thy blade and dudgeon gouts of blood,
Which was not so before. There's no such thing:
It is the bloody business which informs   55
Thus to mine eyes. Now o'er the one half-world
Nature seems dead, and wicked dreams abuse
The curtain'd sleep; witchcraft celebrates
Pale Hecate's offerings; and wither'd murder,
Alarum'd by his sentinel, the wolf,   60
Whose howl's his watch, thus with his stealthy pace,
With Tarquin's ravishing strides, towards his design
Moves like a ghost. Thou sure and firm-set earth,
Hear not my steps, which way they walk, for fear

65   *prate:* talk; that is, reveal

66-67   *take the present horror . . . suits with it:* decrease the terror by breaking the deep and appropriate silence

67   *threat:* threaten

68   *Words . . . breath gives:* talk delays action

70   *knell:* funeral bell

Thy very stones prate of my whereabout,   65
And take the present horror from the time,
Which now suits with it. Whiles I threat, he lives:
Words to the heat of deeds too cold breath gives.

                                                     [*A bell rings*]
I go, and it is done; the bell invites me.
Hear it not, Duncan, for it is a knell   70
That summons thee to heaven, or to hell.   [*Exit*]

Act 2, Scene 1: Activities

1. With a partner, role-play a conversation between Banquo and Fleance in which Fleance questions his father about his (Banquo's) encounter with Macbeth (lines 13–37). What tone would Banquo use?

2. Write a diary entry Macbeth might make about his encounter with Banquo.

3. In a group, decide how Macbeth's soliloquy (lines 40–68) should be acted. As one member of your group reads the soliloquy, the others could recommend what movements, gestures, and facial expressions might be included. Decide whether your performer would see a real dagger, and what lighting and sound effects could be added to achieve the most dramatic atmosphere. Present the performance of the soliloquy to an audience.

4. At the end of his soliloquy just before Macbeth hears the bell ring, he tells himself to stop talking and start doing something. What do you think Macbeth's acknowledged procrastination indicates about the way he is feeling? Think of a time you procrastinated. In your journal, describe the task you kept postponing and what finally prompted you to get on with it.

For the next scene . . .

Think of an action you took and then immediately regretted taking. Why did you regret it? What did you do to make up for your mistake?

Act 2, Scene 2

In this scene . . .

As she waits for her husband to murder the king and return to the courtyard, Lady Macbeth shows that she, too, is very tense. She admits that she needed the help of alcohol and that she was unable to stab Duncan herself. Sounds startle her, but her strength and practicality take control when Macbeth enters in a state of distress. He describes the sounds he heard and imagined he heard and repeats another prophecy-like warning: "Macbeth shall sleep no more." Realizing that he has the bloody daggers with him, Lady Macbeth takes them back to the king's bedchamber. As knocking is heard at the castle entrance, she returns and forces Macbeth to their chamber, so they can both wash their bloody hands and change their clothing.

1 *them:* Duncan's servants

3 *quench'd:* left them unconscious (literally, put out their fire)

5-6 *the fatal bellman . . . good night:* It was believed that the owl was a bird of ill-omen that visited a condemned prisoner on the night before execution.

6 *He is about it:* Macbeth is committing the murder.

7 *surfeited grooms:* drunk servants

8 *do mock their charge with snores:* are making a mockery of their duties by sleeping so heavily

9 *possets:* a night-cap consisting of milk boiled with ale or wine, grated biscuits, eggs, and sugar

10-11 *death and nature . . . live or die:* They are sleeping so deeply that it is hard to tell whether they are dead or alive.

15 *Confounds:* ruins. An unsuccessful attempt would ruin us.

20 *crickets:* The Elizabethans and Jacobeans believed that the chirp of the cricket, like the hoot of the owl, heralded death.

29 *sorry sight:* pitiable, miserable

Scene 2

The same.

Enter Lady Macbeth.

Lady Macbeth: That which hath made them drunk hath
    made me bold;
  What hath quench'd them hath given me fire. Hark!
    Peace!
  It was the owl that shriek'd, the fatal bellman,   5
  Which gives the stern'st good night. He is about it:
  The doors are open, and the surfeited grooms
  Do mock their charge with snores: I have drugg'd their
    possets,
  That death and nature do contend about them,   10
  Whether they live or die.
Macbeth [Within]: Who's there? what, ho!
Lady Macbeth: Alack, I am afraid they have awaked,
  And 'tis not done: the attempt and not the deed
  Confounds us. Hark! I laid their daggers ready;   15
  He could not miss 'em. Had he not resembled
  My father as he slept, I had done't.
  [Enter Macbeth]

                    My husband!
Macbeth: I have done the deed. Didst thou not hear a noise?
Lady Macbeth: I heard the owl scream and the crickets cry.   20
  Did not you speak?
Macbeth   When?
Lady Macbeth: Now.
Macbeth: As I descended?
Lady Macbeth: Ay.   25
Macbeth: Hark!
  Who lies i' the second chamber?
Lady Macbeth: Donalbain.
Macbeth: This is a sorry sight.   *[Looking on his hands]*

34-35   *addressed them/ Again to sleep:* composed themselves and slept again

36   *There are two lodged together:* Lady Macbeth probably means Malcolm and Donalbain.

37   *Amen:* so be it—a solemn statement of consent and affirmation of what has been said

38   *As:* as if; *hangman's hands:* blood-stained, like those of an executioner. In Shakespeare's time, the hangman's hands could well be blood-stained: the bodies of some criminals, especially traitors, were drawn (gutted) and quartered (dismembered) by the executioner.

39   *Listening:* listening to

49   *knits up:* smooths out; *ravell'd:* tangled; *sleave:* a kind of silk. Sleep smooths out the day's problems.

50   *the death of each day's life:* sleep completes the day, as death ends life; *sore labour's bath:* the bath that refreshes the weary worker

51   *Balm:* a soothing ointment; *great nature's second course:* Life is compared to a feast in which the second course, the main dish, is the most nourishing. Thus, day is the first course, night or sleep the second one.

59   *unbend:* relax

60   *brainsickly:* lacking control, feverishly

61   *filthy witness:* evidence

68   *infirm:* weak, unsure

Lady Macbeth: A foolish thought, to say a sorry sight.   30
Macbeth: There's one did laugh in's sleep, and one cried
   "Murder!"
   That they did wake each other; I stood and heard them:
   But they did say their prayers, and addressed them
   Again to sleep.   35
Lady Macbeth: There are two lodged together.
Macbeth: One cried, "God bless us!" and "Amen," the other,
   As they had seen me with these hangman's hands;
   Listening their fear, I could not say, "Amen,"
   When they did say, "God bless us".   40
Lady Macbeth: Consider it not so deeply.
Macbeth: But wherefore could not I pronounce, "Amen"?
   I had most need of blessing, and "Amen"
   Stuck in my throat.
Lady Macbeth: These deeds must not be thought   45
   After these ways; so, it will make us mad.
Macbeth: Methought, I heard a voice cry, "Sleep no more!
   Macbeth does murder sleep"—the innocent sleep,
   Sleep that knits up the ravell'd sleave of care,
   The death of each day's life, sore labour's bath,   50
   Balm of hurt minds, great nature's second course,
   Chief nourisher in life's feast——
Lady Macbeth: What do you mean?
Macbeth: Still it cried, "Sleep no more!" to all the house:
   "Glamis hath murder'd sleep: and therefore Cawdor   55
   Shall sleep no more: Macbeth shall sleep no more!"
Lady Macbeth: Who was it that thus cried? Why, worthy
   thane,
   You do unbend your noble strength, to think
   So brainsickly of things. Go get some water,   60
   And wash this filthy witness from your hand.
   Why did you bring these daggers from the place?
   They must lie there: go carry them, and smear
   The sleepy grooms with blood.
Macbeth: I'll go no more: 65
   I am afraid to think what I have done;
   Look on't again I dare not.
Lady Macbeth: Infirm of purpose!
   Give me the daggers: the sleeping, and the dead

70   *are but as pictures:* have no more life than pictures

70-71   *the eye of childhood . . . devil:* Only children fear a painting of the devil.

72-73   *I'll gild . . . their guilt:* Lady Macbeth's pun on "gild" and "guilt" suggests that guilt is like gilt, a thin overlay of gold, something that can be painted on or washed off.

76   *What hands are here:* Whose hands are these?

76   *they pluck out mine eyes!:* probably an allusion to the New Testament: "And if thine eye cause thee to offend, pluck it out, and cast it from thee . . . " (Mathew xviii, 9)

77   *Neptune:* the Roman god of the sea

79   *multitudinous:* measureless; *incarnadine:* stain red

81   *of your colour:* also covered in blood

86-87   *Your constancy/Hath left you unattended:* Your courage has deserted you.

89-90   *occasion call . . . to be watchers:* in case we are called for and it is obvious that we have not been to bed

90-91   *be not lost/So poorly in your thoughts:* Do not lose yourself in your thoughts.

92   *to know my deed . . . myself:* I would rather be lost in my thoughts than be conscious of what I have done.

Are but as pictures; 'tis the eye of childhood   70
That fears a painted devil. If he do bleed,
I'll gild the faces of the grooms withal,
For it must seem their guilt.   [*Exit. Knocking within*]
Macbeth: Whence is that knocking?
How is't with me, when every noise appals me?   75
What hands are here? Ha! they pluck out mine eyes!
Will all great Neptune's ocean wash this blood
Clean from my hand? No; this my hand will rather
The multitudinous seas incarnadine,
Making the green one red.   80
[*Re-enter Lady Macbeth*]
Lady Macbeth: My hands are of your colour, but I shame
To wear a heart so white. [*Knocking within*] I hear a
    knocking
At the south entry: retire we to our chamber:
A little water clears us of this deed: 85
How easy is it then! Your constancy
Hath left you unattended. [*Knocking within*] Hark, more
    knocking:
Get on your nightgown, lest occasion call us
And show us to be watchers: be not lost   90
So poorly in your thoughts.
Macbeth: To know my deed, 'twere best not know myself.
                              [*Knocking within*]
Wake Duncan with thy knocking! I would thou couldst!
                                  [*Exeunt*]

Act 2, Scene 2: Activities

1. This scene does not show the murder of Duncan. If you had been the author of the play, would you have chosen to include it? Discuss your reasons with your group.

2. In groups, decide how you could shorten this scene by using only the segments you think are most significant. Present your condensed versions to other groups. Compare the versions, discussing which one you think is most effective, and explaining why you think so.

3. As a director of the play, decide what sound effects you would use for this scene. What overall effect would you aim to achieve? Record your ideas in your director's log.

4. What does Macbeth fear most in this scene? What frightens Lady Macbeth? If you were either one of them what would you be most fearful about? With a partner, decide which character you will represent and discuss what you think should most frighten him or her.

For the next scene . . .

Have you ever received an emotional shock? How did you behave immediately afterwards? In what ways did your reaction to the shock change over time?

Act 2, Scene 3

In this scene . . .

The castle porter is awakened from his drunken sleep by the knocking at the castle gates. As he weaves his way across the courtyard, he pretends to be the porter at the gate of hell, admitting those who have committed sins. Eventually he opens the castle gates to Macduff and Lennox, who have been asked by Duncan to awaken him early. Macbeth enters, coming to investigate who has been knocking. After greeting him, Macduff goes to the king's bedchamber while Lennox describes the unnatural disturbances of the night. Macduff returns, announcing hysterically that Duncan has been murdered, and awakens everyone by ordering the alarm bell to be rung. Macbeth and Lennox go to view the murder for themselves and when they return Macbeth reveals that he has killed Duncan's blood-covered grooms, claiming he acted in a loyal rage. On hearing this news, Lady Macbeth faints. The nobles agree to dress and meet as soon as possible to decide on a course of action. However, Duncan's sons, Malcolm and Donalbain, sense danger and plan to slip away quietly and leave the country.

1-2   *porter of hell gate:* The porter is pretending to be the porter at the gate of hell, a traditional figure in medieval miracle plays or religious dramas. He was usually a humorous figure. Shakespeare's audience would have been familiar with his role.

2   *old:* plenty of

4   *Beelzebub:* a devil; *Here's a farmer:* The porter pretends to show in the people waiting at the gate of hell.

5   *hanged himself on the expectation of plenty:* The farmer hoarded corn, believing it would be scarce and the price would increase.Instead, there was a good harvest, so the price of grain fell and he hanged himself.

6   *napkins:* handkerchiefs (to wipe off the sweat of hell)

8   *the other devil's name:* he cannot remember another devil's name

9   *equivocator:* someone who is deliberately ambiguous in order to deceive a listener

9-10   *swear in both the scales against either scale:* commit perjury (Justice is often personified as a figure holding equally balanced scales.)

11   *could not equivocate to heaven:* was not able to talk his way into heaven, despite his skills of deception

14   *for stealing out of a French hose:* The tailor cheated by using less material to make the trousers than he had claimed. As French fashions were not as loose as the English, the trousers were too tight and the theft was discovered.

15   *roast your goose:* the 'goose' was a tailor's iron, with its handle shaped like a goose's neck. Hell would be a good place to heat it.

17   *I'll devil-porter it no further:* I'll stop pretending to be the porter at hell's gate.

19   *the primrose way to the everlasting bonfire:* the pleasant and easy way to destruction and hell. The primrose is a spring flower.

20   *anon:* I'm coming at once

20-21   *remember the/porter:* he asks for a tip

24   *the second cock:* early morning heralded by the crowing of the rooster

25   *provoker:* cause

27   *Marry:* by Mary; an oath expressing mild surprise or indignation; *nose-painting:* drinking alcohol makes the nose red

Scene 3

The same.

Knocking within. Enter a Porter.

Porter: Here's a knocking indeed! If a man were porter of
hell-gate, he should have old turning the key.
[*Knocking within*] Knock, knock, knock! Who's there,
i' the name of Beelzebub? Here's a farmer, that
hanged himself on the expectation of plenty: come in   5
time-server; have napkins enow about you; here you'll
sweat for 't. [*Knocking within*] Knock, knock! Who's
there, in the other devil's name? Faith, here's an
equivocator, that could swear in both the scales against
either scale: who committed treason enough for God's   10
sake, yet could not equivocate to heaven: O, come in,
equivocator. [*Knocking within*] Knock, knock, knock!
Who's there? Faith, here's an English tailor come
hither, for stealing out of a French hose: come in, tailor;
here you may roast your goose. [*Knocking within*]   15
Knock, knock; never at quiet! What are you? But this
place is too cold for hell. I'll devil-porter it no further:
I had thought to have let in some of all professions
that go the primrose way to the everlasting bonfire.
[*Knocking within*] Anon, anon! I pray you, remember the   20
porter. [*Opens the gate*]
[*Enter Macduff and Lennox*]
Macduff: Was it so late, friend, ere you went to bed,
   That you do lie so late?
Porter: 'Faith, sir, we were carousing till the second cock;
   and drink, sir, is a great provoker of three things.   25
Macduff: What three things does drink especially provoke?
Porter: Marry, sir, nose-painting, sleep, and urine. Lechery,
   sir, it provokes and unprovokes: it provokes the
   desire, but it takes away the performance. Therefore,

31   *lechery:* excessive indulgence of sexual desires. The porter describes alcohol as an equivocator because it helps strengthen a man's sexual desires but makes it impossible for him to complete the sexual act.

34-35   *equivocates him in a sleep . . . leaves him:* tricks him into falling asleep, fulfils his desires only in a dream, thereby deceiving him again

34-36   *giving him the lie/drink gave thee the lie last night:* Both the porter and Macduff are punning.

37   *on me:* of me

38   *requited:* paid him back

39   *took up my legs sometime:* made me fall

40   *made a shift:* managed; *cast:* a wrestling term for "throw". To cast can also mean to vomit and to urinate.

47   *timely:* early

48   *slipp'd the hour:* missed the time

52   *physics:* cures

55   *limited service:* appointed duty

58-65   *The night has been unruly . . . and did shake:* Lennox describes a series of abnormal upheavals of nature. Elizabethans and Jacobeans believed that an unnatural event, such as the murder of an anointed king, would be reflected in nature.

58   *lay:* spent the night

60   *lamentings:* moaning

62   *of dire combustion . . . woeful time:* the birth of even more disturbances and confusion

63   *the obscure bird:* the owl, the bird of night which portends death

67-68   *My young remembrance . . . fellow to it:* I have never before, in my short life, experienced a night like this.

much drink may be said to be an equivocator with 30
lechery: it makes him, and it mars him; it sets him
on, and it takes him off; it persuades him, and
disheartens him; makes him stand to, and not stand
to; in conclusion, equivocates him in a sleep, and, giving
him the lie, leaves him. 35

Macduff: I believe, drink gave thee the lie last night.

Porter: That it did, sir, i' the very throat on me: but I
requited him for his lie; and (I think) being too strong
for him, though he took up my legs sometime, yet I
made a shift to cast him. 40

Macduff: Is thy master stirring?
Our knocking has awaked him; here he comes.
[*Enter Macbeth*]

Lennox: Good morrow, noble sir.

Macbeth: Good morrow, both.

Macduff: Is the king stirring, worthy thane? 45

Macbeth: Not yet.

Macduff: He did command me to call timely on him:
I have almost slipp'd the hour.

Macbeth: I'll bring you to him.

Macduff: I know this is a joyful trouble to you; 50
But yet 'tis one.

Macbeth: The labour we delight in physics pain.
This is the door.

Macduff: I'll make so bold to call,
For 'tis my limited service. [*Exit Macduff*] 55

Lennox: Goes the king hence to-day?

Macbeth: He does: he did appoint so.

Lennox: The night has been unruly: where we lay,
Our chimneys were blown down, and, as they say,
Lamentings heard i' the air, strange screams of death, 60
And prophesying with accents terrible
Of dire combustion and confused events
New hatch'd to the woeful time; the obscure bird
Clamour'd the live-long night: some say the earth
Was feverous and did shake. 65

Macbeth: 'Twas a rough night.

Lennox: My young remembrance cannot parallel
A fellow to it.

72   *confusion:* destruction or chaos

73   *sacrilegious:* violating something that is holy or sacred

73-74   *hath broke ope/The Lord's annointed temple:* The Elizabethans
       and Jacobeans believed the king to be chosen by God to be
       his deputy on earth. Thus, the murder of a king was a crime
       against God and humanity.

79   *Gorgon:* The three Gorgons of Greek mythology were hideous
       sisters with hair of writhing snakes. Anyone who looked at them
       would turn to stone. The body of Duncan is just as shocking.

82   *alarum bell:* the great bell of the castle

84   *downy:* soft; *counterfeit:* imitation

86   *The great doom's image:* a likeness of the Day of Judgment

87   *sprites:* spirits. Macduff is continuing the reference to the Day
       of Judgment

90   *hideous trumpet calls to parley:* the clanging bell sounds like a
       trumpet that is calling them to negotiate with an enemy

94-95   *repetition . . . would murder:* a woman could not bear to hear
       the details

103   *chance:* event

[*Re-enter Macduff*]

Macduff: O horror! horror! horror! Tongue, nor heart,
   Cannot conceive, nor name thee!   70

Macbeth, Lennox: What's the matter?

Macduff: Confusion now hath made his master-piece.
   Most sacrilegious murder hath broke ope
   The Lord's anointed temple, and stole thence
   The life o' the building.   75

Macbeth: What is't you say? the life?

Lennox: Mean you his majesty?

Macduff: Approach the chamber, and destroy your sight
   With a new Gorgon: do not bid me speak;
   See, and then speak yourselves.   80
               [*Exeunt Macbeth and Lennox*]
                   Awake! awake!
   Ring the alarum-bell. Murder and treason!
   Banquo and Donalbain! Malcolm! awake!
   Shake off this downy sleep, death's counterfeit,
   And look on death itself! up, up, and see   85
   The great doom's image! Malcolm! Banquo!
   As from your graves rise up, and walk like sprites,
   To countenance this horror! Ring the bell. [*Bell rings*]
   [*Enter Lady Macbeth*]

Lady Macbeth: What's the business,
   That such a hideous trumpet calls to parley   90
   The sleepers of the house? speak, speak!

Macduff: O, gentle lady,
   'Tis not for you to hear what I can speak:
   The repetition, in a woman's ear,
   Would murder as it fell.   95
   [*Enter Banquo*]
                 O Banquo! Banquo!
   Our royal master's murder'd.

Lady Macbeth: Woe, alas!
   What, in our house?

Banquo: Too cruel anywhere. 100
   Dear Duff, I prithee contradict thyself,
   And say it is not so.
   [*Re-enter Macbeth and Lennox*]

Macbeth: Had I but died an hour before this chance.

105   *nothing serious in mortality:* nothing important left in life

106   *toys:* trifles

106   *renown and grace is dead:* Duncan possessed both fame and grace, but they could not save him. His death has made them meaningless.

107-108   *The wine of life . . . to brag of:* The world is a wine cellar from which Duncan, the good wine, has been removed. All we have left to boast about are the dregs, or inferior individuals.

109   *amiss:* wrong

116   *badged:* marked

126   *expedition:* speed

127   *pauser:* delayer. Macbeth claims that his emotions overtook the rational part of him that would have allowed him time to think.

128   *golden blood:* royal blood

129-130   *his gash'd stabs . . . wasteful entrance:* Macbeth compares Duncan's wounded body to a fortress that has been invaded through its broken fortifications.

131   *Steep'd in the colours:* their clothes soaked with blood

132   *unmannerly breech'd with gore:* offensively clothed with clotted blood

132   *refrain:* stop oneself

135   *Help me hence:* Lady Macbeth faints.

138   *that most may claim this argument:* who are the most concerned with this subject

141   *an auger-hole:* a very small hole, made by a carpenter's auger or bore. Donalbain fears that treachery may still be hidden so he and Malcolm are not safe.

I had lived a blessed time; for from this instant
There's nothing serious in mortality; 105
All is but toys: renown and grace is dead;
The wine of life is drawn, and the mere lees
Is left this vault to brag of.
[*Enter Malcolm and Donalbain*]
Donalbain: What is amiss?
Macbeth: You are, and do not know't: 110
  The spring, the head, the fountain of your blood
  Is stopp'd; the very source of it is stopp'd.
Macduff: You royal father's murder'd.
Malcolm: O, by whom?
Lennox: Those of his chamber, as it seemed, had done't; 115
  Their hands and faces were all badged with blood;
  So were their daggers, which unwiped, we found
  Upon their pillows:
  They stared, and were distracted; no man's life
  Was to be trusted with them. 120
Macbeth: O, yet I do repent me of my fury,
  That I did kill them.
Macduff: Wherefore did you so?
Macbeth: Who can be wise, amazed, temperate, and furious,
  Loyal, and neutral, in a moment? No man: 125
  The expedition of my violent love
  Outrun the pauser reason. Here lay Duncan.
  His silver skin laced with his golden blood.
  And his gash'd stabs look'd like a breach in nature
  For ruin's wasteful entrance: there, the murderers, 130
  Steep'd in the colours of their trade, their daggers
  Unmannerly breech'd with gore: who could refrain
  That had a heart to love, and in that heart
  Courage to make's love known?
Lady Macbeth: Help me hence, ho! 135
Macduff: Look to the lady.
Malcolm [*Aside to Donalbain*]: Why do we hold our tongues,
  That most may claim this argument for ours?
Donalbain [*Aside to Malcolm*]: What should be spoken here,
    where our fate, 140
  Hid in an auger-hole, may rush, and seize us?
  Let's away;

143   *brew'd:* surfaced from the depths of sorrow

144-145 *nor our strong . . . of motion:* our deep grief cannot show itself in action yet

147-148 *our naked frailties . . . in exposure:* The aroused sleepers are only scantily clad and are feeling the cold.

150   *scruples:* doubts

152-153 *against the undivulged . . . malice:* I will fight against the secret plans of traitors.

156   *put on manly readiness:* both suitable clothing and attitudes, to prepare for action

159   *consort:* join

160   *office:* duty

164-165 *the near in blood,/The nearer bloody:* The closest relatives are those most likely to murder us.

166-167 *this murderous shaft . . . lighted:* The arrow has not yet hit its target. Malcolm suggests that the murderer will not be satisfied until he has also killed Duncan's sons.

169   *dainty of:* polite in

170   *shift away:* slip away quietly

170-171 *warrant . . . steals itself:* Malcolm puns on "steal", meaning to steal away as well as to commit theft: we can justify stealing away under these circumstances.

Our tears are not yet brew'd.
Malcolm [Aside to Donalbain]:   Nor our strong sorrow
  Upon the foot of motion.   145
Banquo: Look to the lady:
                   [Lady Macbeth is carried out]
  And when we have our naked frailties hid,
  That suffer in exposure, let us meet,
  And question this most bloody piece of work,
  To know it further. Fears and scruples shake us: 150
  In the great hand of God I stand, and thence
  Against the undivulged pretence I fight
  Of treasonous malice.
Macduff: And so do I.
All: So all.   155
Macbeth: Let's briefly put on manly readiness,
  And meet i' the hall together.
All: Well contented.
        [Exeunt all but Malcolm and Donalbain]
Malcolm: What will you do? Let's not consort with them:
  To show an unfelt sorrow is an office   160
  Which the false man does easy. I'll to England.
Donalbain: To Ireland, I: our separated fortune
  Shall keep us both the safer: where we are,
  There's daggers in men's smiles: the near in blood,
  The nearer bloody.   165
Malcolm: This murderous shaft that's shot
  Hath not yet lighted, and our safest way
  Is to avoid the aim. Therefore to horse;
  And let us not be dainty of leave-taking,
  But shift away: there's warrant in that theft   170
  Which steals itself, when there's no mercy left.
                        [Exeunt]

Act 2, Scene 3: Activities

1. Do you think that the drunken porter scene-segment is out of keeping with the rest of the play? As a director, decide whether you would include this part of the scene or cut it, so that the scene would start with Macduff entering at line 45. Discuss your decision with a partner, explaining your reasons.

2. Prepare a dramatization of lines 92–135 in which Lady Macbeth, Malcolm and Donalbain are told about the murder of Duncan and his attendants. Before you present this section, consider the following:
   - How will you ensure that Macbeth, Macduff, and Lennox sound different from each other? What emotional characteristics should make each of their tones different from the other?
   - Will you have Lady Macbeth really faint or simply pretend to do so?

   Present your performance for an audience.

3. In your groups, role-play the court police officer interviewing the prime suspects in Duncan's murder. Determine motives and alibis, and prepare a summary of your conclusions.

4. You are a television reporter who has travelled with the court to cover the royal family's activities for your channel. In the midst of confusion, you are trying to report the story as it happens.
   - Write or tape the opening statements you broadcast to your channel.
   - Then write or tape your revised statement, as you clarify more of the story.
   - Conclude your telecast with a final comment, as the nobles all withdraw to dress and prepare for a council meeting.

5. *Make a video*
   Assume you are the camera operator who accompanies the journalist assigned to cover the royal family. Select one scene you have been able to shoot clearly in the midst of great confusion. Prepare a shooting script or storyboard in which you do the following:
   - Consider the distance between the camera and the subject that would be appropriate for each shot.
   - Consider the camera angle that would be most effective for each shot.
   - Decide on the sequence of shots.
   - Direct how long each shot should last and the speed at which the camera should move from one shot to the other.

   Have other members of your class judge how successful you have been in conveying the drama of the scene.

For the next scene . . .

When do natural events seem *un*natural? In your journal, write about a freakish natural event you have experienced or read about. How did it make you feel?

Act 2, Scene 4

In this scene . . .

In this scene we learn of more *un*natural events that occurred on the night of Duncan's murder. In addition, this is the day following the murder, and the sun has not risen. Macduff tells the Old Man and Ross that the king's sons, who have fled, have been accused of murdering their father. He also reports that Duncan's body has been taken for burial and that Macbeth has been named king. Ross decides to attend Macbeth's coronation, but Macduff refuses and returns home to Fife, hinting that he fears the changes that are happening are not for the better.

1   *threescore and ten:* the Biblical life span

2   *volume:* course

3   *sore:* terrible

4   *trifled former knowings:* made former experiences seem trivial

6   *act:* deed

7   *stage:* world

8   *dark night strangles the travelling lamp:* The sun is not shining.

9   *Is't night's predominance . . . shame:* Has night (associated with evil) defeated day or is day hiding itself in shame for the deeds that have been committed?

10   *entomb:* bury

14   *towering in her pride of place:* circling to reach her highest point

15   *hawk'd at:* attacked like a hawk. In the natural order of things, owls hunt on the ground for mice.

18   *minions of their race:* best of their breed

20   *contending:* struggling

Scene 4

Outside Macbeth's Castle.

Enter Ross and an Old Man.

Old Man: Threescore and ten I can remember well:
　Within the volume of which time I have seen
　Hours dreadful and things strange; but this sore night
　Hath trifled former knowings.
Ross: 　　　　　　　　　Ah, good father,　　　　　5
　Thou see'st, the heavens, as troubled with man's act,
　Threaten his bloody stage: by the clock, 'tis day,
　And yet dark night strangles the travelling lamp:
　Is't night's predominance, or the day's shame,
　That darkness does the face of earth entomb,　　　10
　When living light should kiss it?
Old Man: 　　　　　　　　　　'Tis unnatural,
　Even like the deed that's done. On Tuesday last
　A falcon tow'ring in her pride of place,
　Was by a mousing owl hawk'd at and kill'd.　　　15
Ross: And Duncan's horses—a thing most strange and
　　certain—
　Beauteous and swift, the minions of their race,
　Turn'd wild in nature, broke their stalls, flung out,
　Contending 'gainst obedience, as they would make　20
　War with mankind.
Old Man: 　　　　　　'Tis said they eat each other.
Ross: They did so, to the amazement of mine eyes,
　That look'd upon't.
　[*Enter Macduff*]
　　　　　　　　　Here comes the good Macduff.　25
　How goes the world, sir, now?
Macduff: 　　　　　　　Why, see you not?
Ross: Is't known who did this more than bloody deed?

31   *pretend:* intend, have meant to achieve

32   *suborn'd:* bribed

36   *'Gainst nature still:* more unnatural deeds

37   *Thriftless:* wasteful

37-38 *ravin up/Thine own life's means:* greedily swallow the source of their own lives, and the source from which they would inherit their livelihood (the throne)

40   *Scone:* the ancient royal city, near Perth, where the early Scottish kings were crowned. (See map, page 4.)

41   *invested:* crowned

43   *Colme-kill:* an island in the Hebrides, where many of Scotland's early kings were buried. The island is now called Iona. (See map, page 4.)

44   *storehouse:* tomb

47   *Fife:* Macduff is Thane of Fife, and his castle is there. (See map, page 4.)

48   *thither:* to Scone

50   *sit: fit; lest our old robes . . . sit easier than our new:* in case we find that things are not as good as they used to be

52   *benison:* blessing

53   *That would . . . foes:* those who try to restore order and traditional values

Macduff: Those that Macbeth hath slain.

Ross: Alas, the day! 30
  What good could they pretend?

Macduff: They were suborn'd:
  Malcolm, and Donalbain, the king's two sons,
  Are stol'n away and fled, which puts upon them
  Suspicion of the deed.   35

Ross: 'Gainst nature still:
  Thriftless ambition, that wilt ravin up
  Thine own life's means! Then 'tis most like
  The sovereignty will fall upon Macbeth.

Macduff: He is already named, and gone to Scone   40
  To be invested.

Ross: Where is Duncan's body?

Macduff: Carried to Colme-kill,
  The sacred storehouse of his predecessors,
  And guardian of their bones.   45

Ross: Will you to Scone?

Macduff: No, cousin, I'll to Fife.

Ross: Well, I will thither.

Macduff: Well, may you see things well done there: adieu
  Lest our old robes sit easier than our new!   50

Ross: Farewell, father.

Old Man: God's benison go with you, and with those
  That would make good of bad and friends of foes!

                                                          [*Exeunt*]

Act 2, Scene 4: Activities

1. Write the conversation the Old Man might have with his wife about the encounter with Ross.

2. Some directors have chosen to cut the Old Man from their productions, and start this scene with Ross's greeting to Macduff at line 25. If you were a director, would you? Record the reasons for your decision in your director's log.

Act 2: Consider the Whole Act

1. Recall the moments in this act that you found most memorable. Reread those sections and choose several lines that you think are the most effective. Share them with a partner, explaining why they made a strong impression on you.

2. In your journal, record some of the images and feelings you gained from Act 2. You might use the following to assist you with your response:
   - I saw images of . . .
   - I heard sounds of . . .
   - I wondered why . . .
   - I wonder if . . .

3. Recall the *new* information we have received about both the Macbeths in this act and write it down. Compare what you have written with others' responses.

4. As Lady Macbeth's lady-in-waiting, write a letter to your friend bringing her up to date on events at the castle. Remember that your main interest is in Lady Macbeth and her behaviour. In your letter you might wish to complete the following: "If I were Lady Macbeth I would . . ."

5. As a television reporter, you would like to interview the Scottish nobles before they leave for Macbeth's coronation at Scone. Choose one member of your group to conduct the interviews, while the others take the roles of Macduff, Lennox, Ross, and Banquo. As you conduct the interviews, remember that some nobles may be more open and talkative than others.

6. You are a palace servant who has just been approached by a popular weekly gossip magazine with a cash offer for your "story" about the Macbeths. You cannot resist the offer, but really don't know enough to rely solely on facts. Write a story, being careful not to lie, although you may conjecture or suggest.

7. If, as a news photographer, you could choose only four camera shots that summarize the events in this act, which four would you choose? Compare your choices with those of a partner. Discuss the reasons for your choices.

8. As Malcolm, write a letter to Donalbain sharing your thoughts about the events that have taken place recently in Scotland. Outline what may happen to you and to Scotland in the future.

9. As a television political commentator, write a brief assessment of events in Scotland from the time of the rebellion of Macdonwald until Duncan's death. Consider the king's successes, his errors, and the actions he might have taken to prevent his assassination from occurring.

10. Research the assassination of a twentieth century leader. Consider the motivation for the assassination, the actual assassination, reactions of the public, the appointment of a person to replace the leader, and the identification of the murderer.

    Prepare a report of your findings and present it to your group.

    You could also compare your findings with the murder of Duncan.

For the next scene . . .

Sometimes the failure to speak or act when others expect us to reveal what we know is referred to as a "sin of omission." In your journal, describe a situation in which you were tempted to commit the "sin of omission" or in which you actually did refrain from revealing what you knew. Would you do so again? Explain.

Act 3, Scene 1

In this scene . . .

Macbeth has now taken up residence at Forres. Banquo suspects Macbeth may have murdered Duncan, but he is tempted to remain silent in the hope that the prophecies will be fulfilled for him as they have been for Macbeth. Macbeth makes a formal entry with his retinue and announces a state banquet will be held that night. Banquo tells Macbeth that he will be out horse riding with Fleance until early evening, but he should return in time for the banquet. The retinue exits, leaving Macbeth alone, and we learn that he lacks security in his kingship: he is now obsessed by the witches' prophecies to Banquo. An attendant admits two hired murderers for whom Macbeth has sent. Macbeth convinces them that Banquo is their enemy and deserves to be killed. They agree to murder Banquo and Fleance that evening.

Scene location—*Forres:* Macbeth has taken up residence in Duncan's palace. (See map, page 4.)

4   *stand in thy posterity:* remain in your family

7   *shine:* are brightly fulfilled

8   *verities:* truths

9   *oracles:* prophets

Stage direction—*sennet:* notes played on a trumpet

14   *all-thing:* altogether, completely

15   *solemn supper:* state banquet

15-16   *we hold . . . And I'll request:* When speaking as king, Macbeth uses "we," the royal plural. By using the singular "I'll" and the word "request" he is speaking personally to Banquo.

18-20   *to the which . . . ever knit:* I will always be strongly bound to this command.

24   *Which still hath been both grave and prosperous:* which has always been serious and worthwhile

25   *we'll take tomorrow:* we will have to wait until tomorrow

28-30   *go not my horse the better . . . hour or twain:* If my horse goes no faster than I expect it to, I will have to finish the trip an hour or two after dark.

Act 3, Scene 1

Forres. A room in the Palace.

Enter Banquo.

Banquo: Thou hast it now: king, Cawdor, Glamis, all.
  As the weird women promised; and I fear
  Thou play'dst most foully for't: yet it was said
  It should not stand in thy posterity,
  But that myself should be the root and father   5
  Of many kings. If there come truth from them—
  As upon thee, Macbeth, their speeches shine—
  Why, by the verities on thee made good,
  May they not be my oracles as well
  And set me up in hope? But hush, no more.   10
  [*Sennet sounded. Enter Macbeth, as King; Lady Macbeth*
    as Queen; Lennox, Ross, Lords, Ladies, and Attendants]
Macbeth: Here's our chief guest.
Lady Macbeth: If he had been forgotten
  It had been as a gap in our great feast,
  And all-thing unbecoming.
Macbeth: To-night we hold a solemn supper, sir,   15
  And I'll request your presence.
Banquo: Let your highness
  Command upon me, to the which my duties
  Are with a most indissoluble tie
  For ever knit.   20
Macbeth: Ride you this afternoon?
Banquo: Ay, my good lord.
Macbeth: We should have else desired your good advice
  Which still hath been both grave and prosperous
  In this day's council; but we'll take to-morrow.   25
  Is't far you ride?
Banquo: As far, my lord, as will fill up the time
  'Twixt this and supper: go not my horse the better,

33   *bloody:* guilty; *bestow'd:* settled

35   *parricide:* murder of one's father

36   *strange invention:* telling lies or tales they have invented

37-38   *When therewithal . . . us jointly:* when affairs of state will require attention from both of us

40   *our time does call:* it is time for us to go

44   *master of his time:* do as he wishes with his time

45   *society:* company

47   *while:* until

48   *sirrah:* term used by a person of authority to address a social inferior, or by an adult addressing a boy

50   *without:* outside

52   *to be thus:* to be king

53   *but to be safely thus:* the necessary thing is to reign in security

54-55   *in his royalty of nature . . . be fear'd:* Macbeth admires Banquo's noble character but he also fears it, perhaps because Macbeth suffers by comparison, or perhaps because he believes Banquo's honesty will lead him to expose Macbeth.

56   *to that:* in addition to; *dauntless:* fearless

59   *being:* existence

60   *genius:* guardian spirit. Macbeth means that he feels inferior when he compares himself with Banquo. The Roman Mark Antony apparently felt similarly inferior to Octavius Caesar.

61   *chid:* scolded, rebuked

65   *fruitless:* childless

66   *sceptre:* a symbol of kingship; *gripe:* grasp

67   *with an unlineal hand:* by a person not of my family

I must become a borrower of the night,
For a dark hour or twain.   30
Macbeth: Fail not our feast.
Banquo: My lord, I will not.
Macbeth: We hear, our bloody cousins are bestow'd
   In England and in Ireland, not confessing
   Their cruel parricide, filling their hearers   35
   With strange invention: but of that to-morrow,
   When therewithal we shall have cause of state
   Craving us jointly. Hie you to horse: adieu,
   Till you return at night. Goes Fleance with you?
Banquo: Ay, my good lord: our time does call upon us. 40
Macbeth: I wish your horses swift and sure of foot,
   And so I do commend you to their backs.
   Farewell.   [*Exit Banquo*]
   Let every man be master of his time
   Till seven at night; to make society   45
   The sweeter welcome, we will keep ourself
   Till supper-time alone: while then, God be with you!
          [*Exeunt all but Macbeth and an Attendant*]
   Sirrah, a word with you: attend those men
   Our pleasure?
Attendant: They are, my lord, without the palace-gate. 50
Macbeth: Bring them before us.   [*Exit Attendant*]
                    To be thus, is nothing;
   But to be safely thus: our fears in Banquo
   Stick deep; and in his royalty of nature
   Reigns that which would be fear'd: 'tis much he dares, 55
   And, to that dauntless temper of his mind,
   He hath a wisdom that doth guide his valour
   To act in safety. There is none but he
   Whose being I do fear; and under him
   My genius is rebuked, as it is said   60
   Mark Antony's was by Cæsar. He chid the sisters,
   When first they put the name of king upon me,
   And bade them speak to him; then prophet-like
   They hail'd him father to a line of kings:
   Upon my head they placed a fruitless crown,   65
   And put a barren sceptre in my gripe,
   Thence to be wrench'd with an unlineal hand,

69   *issue:* offspring; *filed:* defiled, corrupted

70   *gracious:* full of religious grace

71   *rancours:* malice, bitterness. Macbeth is no longer at peace
      with himself. The metaphor suggests that his peace of mind was
      enclosed in a sacred container into which a corrupting
      substance has been introduced.

72   *mine eternal jewel:* immortal soul

73   *the common enemy of man:* the devil, Satan

74   *seed:* descendants

75   *list:* an arena in which medieval knights held tilting contests.
      Two armed opponents would compete to knock each other off
      their horses.

76   *utterance:* death.

82   *he:* Banquo

82-83 *held you so under fortune:* kept you down below where you
      deserve to be

83-84 *you thought . . . innocent self:* You had, incorrectly, blamed me.

84   *made good:* showed you clearly

85   *pass'd in probation with you:* proved to you

86   *borne in hand:* deceived; *cross'd:* defeated

87   *the instruments:* the means used

88   *wrought:* worked

89   *half a soul:* a half-wit; *notion:* mind

95   *so gospell'd:* so influenced by the teachings of the gospel (that
      is, forgiveness)

98   *yours:* your families

100   *the catalogue:* the list. This general list or classification of living
      things is in contrast with the "valued file" (line 103) which de-
      fines the special qualities of those listed.

102   *shoughs:* shaggy dogs; *water-rugs:* rough-haired water dogs;
      demi-wolves: a cross between a dog and a wolf; *clept:* called

105   *housekeeper:* watch dog

No son of mine succeeding. If't be so,
For Banquo's issue have I filed my mind;
For them the gracious Duncan have I murder'd;　　　70
Put rancours in the vessel of my peace
Only for them; and mine eternal jewel
Given to the common enemy of man,
To make them kings, the seed of Banquo kings!
Rather than so, come, fate, into the list,　　　75
And champion me to the utterance! Who's there?
[Re-enter Attendant, with two Murderers]
Now go to the door, and stay there till we call.
　　　　　　　　　　　　　　　　[Exit Attendant]
Was it not yesterday we spoke together?
First Murderer: It was, so please your highness.
Macbeth:　　　　　　　　　　　　Well then, now　80
Have you consider'd of my speeches? Know
That it was he in the times past which held you
So under fortune, which you thought had been
Our innocent self: this I made good to you
In our last conference; pass'd in probation with you,　　　85
How you were borne in hand, how cross'd, the
　　instruments,
Who wrought with them; and all things else that might
To half a soul and to a notion crazed
Say, "Thus did Banquo".　　　90
First Murderer:　　　　　　　You made it known to us.
Macbeth: I did so; and went further, which is now
Our point of second meeting. Do you find
Your patience so predominant in your nature,
That you can let this go? Are you so gospell'd,　　　95
To pray for this good man and for his issue,
Whose heavy hand hath bow'd you to the grave
And beggar'd yours for ever?
First Murderer:　　　　　　　We are men, my liege.
Macbeth: Ay, in the catalogue ye go for men;　　　100
As hounds, and greyhounds, mongrels, spaniels, curs,
Shoughs, water-rugs, and demi-wolves, are clept
All by the name of dogs: the valued file
Distinguishes the swift, the slow, the subtle,
The housekeeper, the hunter, every one　　　105

107   *closed:* enclosed, set

108   *particular addition:* a title that distinguishes him

110-111 *if you have a station . . . rank of manhood:* Macbeth invites the men to remove themselves from the general list, to place themselves on the special list, and thus to rise from the lowest level of humanity.

112   *put that business in your bosoms:* confide my plans to you

114   *grapples:* brings you close

115-116 *who wear our health . . . were perfect:* While he lives I am not well; when he dies I will be healthy.

117   *liege:* lord

119   *incensed:* angered

122   *tugg'd with:* knocked about by

123   *set:* gamble

124   *mend:* improve; *rid:* lose

128   *bloody distance:* dangerous relationship. "Distance" is a fencing term for the space between two opponents.

130   *my near'st of life:* my very life

132   *bid my will avouch it:* justify it by saying I wished to do so

134   *may not:* cannot; *but wail his fall:* but I must mourn his death

136   *do make love:* appeal to you

137   *common eye:* the people

142   *spirits:* courage

145   *the perfect spy o' the time:* the very best time, as based on information obtained

According to the gift which bounteous nature
Hath in him closed, whereby he does receive
Particular addition, from the bill
That writes them all alike; and so of men.
Now if you have a station in the file,   110
Not in the worst rank of manhood, say it,
And I will put that business in your bosoms
Whose execution takes your enemy off,
Grapples you to the heart and love of us,
Who wear our health but sickly in his life,   115
Which in his death were perfect.
Second Murderer: I am one, my liege:
Whom the vile blows and buffets of the world
Have so incensed, that I am reckless what
I do to spite the world.   120
First Murderer: And I another
So weary with disasters, tugg'd with fortune,
That I would set my life on any chance,
To mend it or be rid on't.
Macbeth: Both of you   125
Know Banquo was your enemy.
Second Murderer: True, my lord.
Macbeth: So is he mine, and in such bloody distance,
That every minute of his being thrusts
Against my near'st of life: and though I could   130
With barefaced power sweep him from my sight
And bid my will avouch it, yet I must not,
For certain friends that are both his and mine,
Whose loves I may not drop, but wail his fall
Who I myself struck down: and thence it is   135
That I to your assistance do make love—
Masking the business from the common eye
For sundry weighty reasons.
Second Murderer: We shall, my lord,
Perform what you command us.   140
First Murderer: Though our lives——
Macbeth: Your spirits shine through you. Within this hour
    at most
I will advise you where to plant yourselves,
Acquaint you with the perfect spy o' the time,   145

147   *always thought:* let it be understood

148   *a clearness:* to be clear of any blame

149   *no rubs nor botches:* difficulties and mistakes

151   *absence:* euphemism for death

151   *material:* important

153   *Resolve yourselves apart:* come to a decision in private

154   *anon:* immediately

156   *straight:* immediately

The moment on't; for't must be done to-night,
And something from the palace; always thought
That I require a clearness. And with him—
To leave no rubs nor botches in the work—
Fleance his son, that keeps him company,   150
Whose absence is no less material to me
Than is his father's, must embrace the fate
Of that dark hour. Resolve yourselves apart;
I'll come to you anon.
Second Murderer: We are resolved, my lord.   155
Macbeth: I'll call upon you straight; abide within.
                                        [*Exeunt Murderers*]
It is concluded: Banquo, thy soul's flight,
If it find heaven, must find it out to-night.
                                        [*Exeunt*]

Act 3, Scene 1: Activities

1. With your group, discuss whether Banquo is prepared to wait for the prophecies to be fulfilled, or whether he might want to help them along. Rehearse a presentation of Banquo's soliloquy for an audience.

2. Plan and rehearse a production of the court scene (lines 11–47), remembering that it is a large and formal gathering, and that Macbeth wants all present to hear his conversation with Banquo. Consider the following as you undertake the project:

   Step 1: *Blocking*
   Decide upon appropriate stage positions for all of the characters in the scene. Where will they stand? When, where, and how will they move?

   Step 2: *Rehearsing*
   Put movements and lines together. Adjust stage positions and movements as well as line delivery. Work for freshness, spontaneity, and dramatic impact.

   Step 3: *Using effects*
   Choose appropriate sound and lighting effects.

   Step 4: *Presenting*
   Perform your scene. Discuss with your audience their reactions.

3. As a friend of Banquo present at this scene, you begin to worry about his safety. Choose and prepare the best way of warning him. You may wish to write a letter, script a conversation, or devise another form of warning.

4. a) In his soliloquy, Macbeth explains his reasons for deciding to have Banquo murdered. What impressions of Macbeth do you gain from learning about this reasoning process?

b) Do you think his ploy for avoiding the guilt of murdering Banquo and Fleance will be successful? Explain your response.

5. Discuss with a partner the arguments and techniques Macbeth uses to convince the murderers to kill Banquo and Fleance. Consider why he bothers to persuade them when he could just give the order and promise to pay them well.

6. Macbeth tells the murderers to make up their minds in private. With your partner, role-play the conversation in which the murderers decide to kill Banquo.

7. Imagine you are the court psychologist counselling Macbeth. Write two reports, the first to keep in an official file for Macbeth's use and the second for your private file.

For the next scene . . .

Sometimes, achieving a goal we have longed for does not make us feel as happy as we expected. Why do you think this is so? Share your ideas with others.

Act 3, Scene 2

In this scene . . .

Lady Macbeth expresses her unhappiness but, when Macbeth enters, she resumes her role as the practical advisor. We learn that both she and Macbeth are suffering from troubled sleep, nightmares, and loss of appetite. They determine to hide their agitation and to be welcoming and jovial at their banquet. Macbeth hints to Lady Macbeth that he has made plans for some significant action, but he refuses to give her any details.

6   *nought's had, all's spent:* nothing is gained, everything is lost

11   *sorriest fancies:* wretched imaginings

12   *Using:* harbouring

13   *them:* his victims

13-14   *things without all . . . without regard:* Problems that cannot be
        resolved should be ignored.

15   *scotch'd:* slashed

16   *close:* heal; *poor:* weak

17   *former tooth:* Macbeth's image is of a snake bite. Macbeth, in
        other words, feels insecure in his hold on the crown.

18   *the frame of things . . . worlds suffer:* Let the universe, both
        heaven and earth, fall to pieces.

22   *to gain our peace have sent to peace:* Macbeth puns. For his
        own peace of mind, to satisfy his ambition, he has sent Duncan
        to eternal peace.

23   *the torture of the mind:* The image is of a rack, on which the
        victim was bound and stretched.

24   *ecstasy:* a frenzied state of mind, not necessarily caused by
        joy, as in the usual modern usage.

27   *malice domestic:* civil war or, perhaps, treason; *foreign levy:*
        the invasion of a foreign army

Scene 2

The Palace.

*Enter Lady Macbeth and a
Servant.*

Lady Macbeth: Is Banquo gone from court?
Servant: Ay, madam, but returns again to-night.
Lady Macbeth: Say to the king, I would attend his leisure
   For a few words.
Servant: Madam, I will.   *[Exit]*   5
Lady Macbeth: Nought's had, all's spent.
   Where our desire is got without content:
   'Tis safer to be that which we destroy
   Than, by destruction, dwell in doubtful joy.
   [Enter Macbeth]
   How now, my lord? why do you keep alone,   10
   Of sorriest fancies your companions making;
   Using those thoughts which should indeed have died
   With them they think on? Things without all remedy
   Should be without regard: what's done is done.
Macbeth: We have scotch'd the snake, not kill'd it;   15
   She'll close and be herself, whilst our poor malice
   Remains in danger of her former tooth.
   But let the frame of things disjoint, both the worlds suffer,
   Ere we will eat our meal in fear, and sleep
   In the affliction of these terrible dreams   20
   That shake us nightly: better be with the dead,
   Whom we, to gain our peace, have sent to peace,
   Than on the torture of the mind to lie
   In restless ecstasy. Duncan is in his grave,
   After life's fitful fever he sleeps well,   25
   Treason has done his worst: nor steel, nor poison,
   Malice domestic, foreign levy, nothing,
   Can touch him further!

30   *sleek o'er your rugged looks:* look relaxed and happy

33   *Let your remembrance apply:* remember to pay special attention

34   *Present him eminence:* single him out for the greatest honour

36   *lave:* wash; *must lave our honours in these flattering streams:* The metaphor suggests that, to remain in power, they have to depend on flattery.

37   *vizards:* the visor of the helmet, which serves as a mask of protection

39   *You must leave this:* dismiss such thoughts

42   *in them nature's copy's not eterne:* Banquo and Fleance are not immortal.

43   *they are assailable:* they can be attacked

44   *jocund:* joyful, merry

46   *shard:* scaly wings. The beetle flies at night, so its humming signals night-fall.

48   *note:* notoriety

50   *dearest chuck:* a term of endearment, probably from "chick"

51   *seeling:* dark. To seel was to sew up the eyelids of a falcon which was easier to tame when it could not see. Once tamed, it could be trained for hunting.

52   *scarf:* blindfold. Macbeth calls on night to fall so darkness will hide his deed.

53   *bloody and invisible hand:* covered with blood from the seeling and now invisible to the falcon.

54   *that great bond:* Banquo's life, seen as a legal agreement between Banquo and nature.

55   *keeps me pale:* holds me back. A pale is a pointed piece of wood used to build a fence. Macbeth may also mean pale with fear; *Light thickens:* grows denser, that is, darkens

56   *rooky:* filled with rooks or crows

58   *night's black agents to their preys do rouse:* evil begins to hunt for its victims

60   *things bad begun . . . by ill:* Evil deeds grow stronger with more evil deeds.

Lady Macbeth: Come on;
 Gentle my lord, sleek o'er your rugged looks;   30
 Be bright and jovial among your guests to-night.
Macbeth: So shall I, love; and so, I pray, be you:
 Let your remembrance apply to Banquo:
 Present him eminence, both with eye and tongue:
 Unsafe the while, that we   35
 Must lave our honours in these flattering streams,
 And make our faces vizards to our hearts,
 Disguising what they are.
Lady Macbeth: You must leave this.
Macbeth: O, full of scorpions is my mind, dear wife!   40
 Thou know'st that Banquo, and his Fleance, lives.
Lady Macbeth: But in them nature's copy's not eterne.
Macbeth: There's comfort yet; they are assailable;
 Then be thou jocund: ere the bat hath flown
 His cloister'd flight; ere to black Hecate's summons   45
 The shard-borne beetle, with his drowsy hums,
 Hath rung night's yawning peal, there shall be done
 A deed of dreadful note.
Lady Macbeth: What's to be done?
Macbeth: Be innocent of the knowledge, dearest chuck,   50
 Till thou applaud the deed. Come, seeling night,
 Scarf up the tender eye of pitiful day,
 And with thy bloody and invisible hand,
 Cancel and tear to pieces that great bond
 Which keeps me pale! Light thickens, and the crow   55
 Makes wing to the rooky wood;
 Good things of day begin to droop and drowse,
 Whiles night's black agents to their preys do rouse.
 Thou marvell'st at my words: but hold thee still;
 Things bad begun make strong themselves by ill: 60
 So, prithee, go with me.   [*Exeunt*]

Act 3, Scene 2: Activities

1. Lady Macbeth is finding that the murder of Duncan has not brought the happiness she had expected. Write a short soliloquy Lady Macbeth might add after line 9 in which she explains what she had hoped life would be like once she became Queen of Scotland.

2. Before meeting with his wife, Macbeth probably decided he would not tell her his plan for killing Banquo and Fleance. Why do you think he made this decision?
   With a partner, discuss the ways in which the Macbeths' marriage seems to be changing. In your opinion, is this a weakening or a strengthening of their relationship?

3. Select the image in this scene that you find the most powerful and memorable. Write the quotation in your notebook and then complete one of the following:
   This image makes me see . . .
   This image makes me feel . . .
   Explain the reasons for its effect and share your response with your group.
   You may prefer to prepare an illustration of the image.

4. In your journal, write your response to either Lady Macbeth's advice, "Things without all remedy/Should be without regard: what's done is done" or to Macbeth's statement, "Things bad begun make strong themselves by ill."

For the next scene . . .

Have you ever known or read about someone who was distrustful of everybody and everything, regardless of the circumstances or evidence? Why was this person so suspicious? What effect did this attitude have on others?

Act 3, Scene 3

In this scene . . .

As they wait in the early evening for Banquo and
Fleance to pass by, the two murderers are joined by
a third. It appears he has been sent by Macbeth who
no longer trusts anybody. When Banquo and Fleance
arrive, carrying a torch, one murderer puts out the
light and the other two stab Banquo. In the darkness
Fleance escapes.

3 *He needs not our mistrust . . . just:* We need not be suspicious of him since he already knows why we are here.

8 *'lated:* belated, late

9 *To gain the timely inn:* to reach the inn in good time (before dark)

12 *Give us a light:* Banquo is calling to the palace grooms

14 *within the note of expectation:* on the list of expected guests

16 *His horses go about:* The grooms are taking the horses around to the stables

22 *Stand to't:* keep firm

Scene 3

*A park or lawn, with a gate leading
to the Palace.*

Enter three Murderers.

First Murderer: But who did bid thee join with us!
Third Murderer: Macbeth.
Second Murderer: He needs not our mistrust; since he delivers
  Our offices, and what we have to do,
  To the direction just.   5
First Murderer: Then stand with us.
  The west yet glimmers with some streaks of day.
  Now spurs the 'lated traveller apace
  To gain the timely inn; and near approaches
  The subject of our watch.   10
Third Murderer: Hark! I hear horses.
Banquo [*Within*]: Give us a light there, ho!
Second Murderer: Then 'tis he; the rest
  That are within the note of expectation
  Already are i' the court.   15
First Murderer: His horses go about.
Third Murderer: Almost a mile; but he does usually—
  So all men do—from hence to the palace gate
  Make it their walk.
Second Murderer: A light, a light!   20
  [*Enter Banquo, and Fleance with a torch*]
Third Murderer: 'Tis he.
First Murderer: Stand to't.
Banquo: It will be rain to-night.
First Murderer: Let it come down.
                [*Assaults Banquo*]
Banquo: O, treachery! Fly, good Fleance, fly, fly, fly!   25
  Thou mayst revenge. O slave!
            [*Dies. Fleance escapes*]

28   *Was't not the way:* was it not the thing to do?

Third Murderer: Who did strike out the light?
First Murderer: Was't not the way?
Third Murderer: There's but one down; the son is fled.
Second Murderer: We have lost   30
    Best half of our affair.
First Murderer: Well, let's away, and say how much is
    done.   [*Exeunt*]

Act 3, Scene 3: Activities

1. In a group, role-play the murderers' conversation as they imagine what Macbeth will say to them when he hears that Fleance has escaped. What fate might they expect?

2. Conduct an informal debate on the topic, "Banquo deserved this death."

3. Write either the obituary for Banquo that will appear in Scotland's national newspaper or the leading article reporting the discovery of Banquo's body.

4. As Fleance, write a letter to your mother saying you are well and explaining how you escaped.

For the next scene . . .

Describe the most frightening experience you ever had. What was the cause of your fear?

Act 3, Scene 4

In this scene . . .

The Macbeths formally welcome their guests to the banquet. Macbeth prepares to drink to their health, but glimpses one of the murderers at the door. When he is informed of Fleance's escape he is, of course, very upset, but is called back by his wife to his duties as host. As he prepares to join his guests at the table, he comments on how disappointed he is that Banquo is not present. As if in answer, the murdered man's ghost enters and sits at the table. The guests, who do not see the ghost, are startled by Macbeth's horrified reaction. Lady Macbeth tries to calm him with appeals to his manliness, his common sense and, finally, to his role as host. When the ghost disappears, the Macbeths blame his behaviour on poor health. Foolishly, Macbeth calls for a toast to the absent Banquo, who immediately reappears. Macbeth's ravings betray so much that Lady Macbeth hastily asks the guests to leave. As Lady Macbeth wearily tries to comfort her husband, Macbeth reveals that he is angry at Macduff and plans to visit the witches again. He comforts himself with the thought that more experience will prepare him to deal better with the horrors he has created.

1   *degrees:* rank. At a formal banquet, the guests would sit in order of rank.

6   *keeps her state:* remains in her chair of state.

10   *they encounter thee:* they respond to you

11   *Both sides . . . the midst:* As there are equal numbers of guests on both sides of the table, Macbeth chooses to sit in the middle, that is, to "mingle".

12   *a measure:* a toast

16   *'Tis better thee . . . he within:* It is better that the blood is on you than in Banquo's veins.

17   *despatch'd:* sent away—a euphemism for killed

21   *nonpareil:* without equal

24   *my fit:* the fever or spasm of fear

25   *perfect:* completely happy

Scene 4

*A room of state in the Palace. A
Banquet prepared.*

*Enter Macbeth, Lady Macbeth,
Ross, Lennox, Lords and
Attendants.*

Macbeth: You know your own degrees; sit down: at first
 And last the hearty welcome.
Lords: Thanks to your majesty.
Macbeth: Ourself will mingle with society
 And play the humble host.   5
 Our hostess keeps her state, but in best time
 We will require her welcome.
Lady Macbeth: Pronounce it for me, sir, to all our friends,
 For my heart speaks they are welcome.
 [*Enter first Murderer to the door*]
Macbeth: See, they encounter thee with their hearts' thanks.   10
 Both sides are even: here I'll sit i' the midst:
 Be large in mirth; anon we'll drink a measure
 The table round. [*Approaching the door*] There's blood
  upon thy face.
Murderer: 'Tis Banquo's then.   15
Macbeth: 'Tis better thee without, than he within.
 Is he despatch'd?
Murderer: My lord, his throat is cut; that I did for him.
Macbeth: Thou art the best o' the cut-throats: yet he's good
 That did the like for Fleance: if thou didst it,   20
 Thou art the nonpareil.
Murderer: Most royal, sir,
 Fleance is 'scaped.
Macbeth [*Aside*]: Then comes my fit again: I had else been
  perfect,   25

141

26 *Whole:* sound; *founded:* immovable

27 *As broad and general as the casing air:* as free and unconfined as the air around me

28 *cabin'd:* shut up, as in a small cabin

29 *saucy:* insolent, intrusive

32 *The least a death to nature:* each enough to have killed someone

34 *the worm:* little serpent (used often by Elizabethan writers to mean a serpent)

37 *No teeth for the present:* Though Fleance will grow into an enemy, he is no threat at present.

38 *hear ourselves:* talk together

40 *give the cheer:* entertain the guests

40-42 *the feast is sold . . . welcome:* Unless the host assures his guests that they are welcome, they might as well be eating a meal for which they have to pay; *to feed:* simply to eat.

43 *the sauce to meat is ceremony:* Entertainment and company are the best part of a meal.

49 *our country's honour roof'd:* All Scotland's nobility would be here under one roof.

51-52 *Who may I rather challenge . . . for mischance:* I hope that I am right to reprimand Banquo for his lack of courtesy, rather than pity him because he has had some accident.

54 *Lays blame upon:* means he did not keep

56 *The table's full:* Only Macbeth can see Banquo's ghost.

61 *Which of you have done this?:* He thinks at first that the ghost is some kind of practical joke.

63 *Thou canst not say I did it:* Macbeth claims that he cannot be blamed, as he did not do the killing himself.

64 *gory:* bloody

Whole as the marble, founded as the rock,
As broad and general as the casing air:
But now I am cabin'd, cribb'd, confined, bound in
To saucy doubts and fears. But Banquo's safe?
Murderer: Ay, my good lord: safe in a ditch he bides,   30
With twenty trenched gashes on his head;
The least a death to nature.
Macbeth: Thanks for that.
[*Aside*] There the grown serpent lies: the worm that's
    fled   35
Hath nature that in time will venom breed,
No teeth for the present. Get thee gone; to-morrow
We'll hear ourselves again.   [*Exit Murderer*]
Lady Macbeth: My royal lord,
You do not give the cheer: the feast is sold   40
That is not often vouch'd, while 'tis a making,
'Tis given with welcome: to feed were best at home;
From thence the sauce to meat is ceremony;
Meeting were bare without it.
Macbeth: Sweet remembrancer!   45
Now good digestion wait on appetite,
And health on both!
Lennox: May it please your highness, sit?
Macbeth: Here had we now our country's honour roof'd,
Were the grac'd person of our Banquo present;   50
[*Enter the Ghost of Banquo and sits in Macbeth's place*]
Who may I rather challenge for unkindness
Than pity for mischance!
Ross: His absence, sir,
Lays blame upon his promise. Please't your highness
To grace us with your royal company.   55
Macbeth: The table's full.
Lennox: Here is a place reserved, sir.
Macbeth: Where?
Lennox: Here, my good lord. What is't that moves your
    highness?   60
Macbeth: Which of you have done this?
Lords: What, my good lord?
Macbeth: Thou canst not say I did it: never shake
Thy gory locks at me.

68   *upon a thought:* in an instant

70   *extend his passion:* make him worse, prolong his suffering

74   *proper stuff:* absolute nonsense

75   *the very painting of your fear:* It is an image conjured up by your fear.

76   *the air-drawn dagger:* drawn through the air or created (sketched) out of air

77   *flaws and starts:* sudden outbursts

78   *imposters to true fear:* false when compared with genuine fear

79   *A woman's story . . . grandam:* Macbeth's behaviour is like that of a superstitious old woman.

85   *charnel-houses:* vaults in which dead bodies and dried bones were kept.

86-87 *our monuments . . . kites:* we will have to leave their bodies to be eaten by birds of prey.

88   *unmann'd in folly:* your foolishness has destroyed your manhood

92   *Ere human statute purged the gentle weal:* before the laws of civilized society put an end to violence

97   *With twenty mortal murders on their crowns:* with twenty fatal wounds on their heads. At one time, when stabbed in the head, a man would die. But now a man covered with fatal wounds returns from the dead

101   *do lack you:* need your company

103   *muse:* wonder

Ross: Gentlemen, rise; his highness is not well. 65
Lady Macbeth: Sit, worthy friends: my lord is often thus,
  And hath been from his youth: 'pray you, keep seat;
  The fit is momentary; upon a thought
  He will again be well. If much you note him,
  You shall offend him, and extend his passion; 70
  Feed, and regard him not. Are you a man?
Macbeth: Ay, and a bold one, that dare look on that
  Which might appal the devil.
Lady Macbeth: O proper stuff!
  This is the very painting of your fear: 75
  This is the air-drawn dagger which, you said,
  Led you to Duncan. O, these flaws and starts,
  Impostors to true fear, would well become
  A woman's story at a winter's fire,
  Authorised by her grandam. Shame itself! 80
  Why do you make such faces? When all's done,
  You look but on a stool.
Macbeth: Prithee, see there! behold! look! lo! how say you?
  Why, what care I? If thou canst nod, speak too.
  If charnel-houses and our graves must send 85
  Those that we bury back, our monuments
  Shall be the maws of kites.   [*Exit Ghost*]
Lady Macbeth: What? quite unmann'd in folly?
Macbeth: If I stand here, I saw him.
Lady Macbeth: Fie, for shame! 90
Macbeth: Blood hath been shed ere now, i' the olden time,
  Ere human statute purged the gentle weal;
  Ay, and since too, murders have been performed
  Too terrible for the ear: the time has been,
  That when the brains were out, the man would die, 95
  And there an end: but now, they rise again,
  With twenty mortal murders on their crowns,
  And push us from our stools: this is more strange
  Than such a murder is.
Lady Macbeth: My worthy lord, 100
  Your noble friends do lack you.
Macbeth: I do forget.
  Do not muse at me, my most worthy friends;
  I have a strange infirmity, which is nothing

110 *to all and him we thirst:* we drink to all of you and to Banquo

112 *our duties and the pledge:* we toast our homage and allegiance to you

113 *Avaunt:* Go away!

116 *speculation:* intelligence

119 *a thing of custom:* a regular event; *'tis no other:* it is nothing else

123 *the arm'd rhinoceros:* horned and with a hide like armour; *the Hyrcan tiger:* the fiercest tigers, it was believed, came from Hyrcania, near the Caspian Sea

124 *but that:* of Banquo

126 *dare me to the desert:* challenge me to fight in any deserted place

127 *If trembling I inhabit then:* if I tremble, live in fear; *protest:* call

128 *the baby of a girl:* a girl's doll, or a baby girl

134 *most admired disorder:* most amazing lack of self-control

136 *overcome:* pass over

137-138 *You make me strange/ Even to . . . that I owe:* You make me feel like a stranger to myself. Macbeth is amazed that Lady Macbeth appears to be unmoved by a sight that has terrified him. He wonders if he is really as brave as he has always thought himself to be.

141 *blanch'd:* white

To those that know me. Come, love and health to all: 105
Then I'll sit down. Give me some wine, fill full.
I drink to the general joy of the whole table,
And to our dear friend Banquo, whom we miss:
Would he were here!
[*Re-enter Ghost*]   To all and him we thirst,   110
And all to all.
Lords: Our duties, and the pledge.
Macbeth: Avaunt! and quit my sight! Let the earth hide
    thee!
Thy bones are marrowless, thy blood is cold;   115
Thou hast no speculation in those eyes
Which thou dost glare with.
Lady Macbeth: Think of this, good peers,
But as a thing of custom: 'tis no other;
Only it spoils the pleasure of the time.   120
Macbeth: What man may dare, I dare:
Approach thou like the rugged Russian bear,
The arm'd rhinoceros, or the Hyrcan tiger;
Take any shape but that, and my firm nerves
Shall never tremble: or be alive again,   125
And dare me to the desert with thy sword;
If trembling I inhabit then, protest me
The baby of a girl. Hence, horrible shadow!
Unreal mockery, hence!   *[Ghost disappears]*
    Why, so; being gone,   130
I am a man again. Pray you, sit still.
Lady Macbeth: You have displaced the mirth, broke the
    good meeting,
With most admired disorder.
Macbeth: Can such things be,   135
And overcome us like a summer's cloud,
Without our special wonder? You make me strange
Even to the disposition that I owe,
When now I think you can behold such sights,
And keep the natural ruby of your cheeks,   140
When mine is blanch'd with fear.
Ross: What sights, my lord?
Lady Macbeth: I pray you, speak not; he grows worse and
    worse;

146-147   *Stand not . . . at once:* do not take the time to leave in order of rank

151   *It:* the murder of Banquo; *blood will have blood:* a murderer will be exposed and killed.

153   *Augures:* prophecies; *understood relations:* connections between events

154   *By magot-pies . . . brought forth:* have been revealed by magpies and crows. Macbeth maintains that the elements of nature will somehow expose even the most secretive of murders.

155   *What is the night?:* What time is it?

158   *How say'st thou:* what do you think about the fact; *denies his person:* refuses to come

161   *I hear it by the way:* I've heard it informally

162-163   *There's not a one . . . a servant fee'd:* In every noble's house I pay a servant to spy for me.

165   *bent:* determined

166   *the worst:* the worst information or news

167   *All causes shall give way:* Everything else must take second place.

167-169   *I am in blood . . . go o'er:* The image pictures Macbeth wading in a river of blood, having proceeded so far that it is easier to continue than try to return to the starting point.

170-171   *Strange things . . . may be scann'd:* I will do without any contemplation, the things that come into my mind. (The metaphor is from acting: the actor must perform the part without first learning it.)

172   *the season:* the seasoning, a preservative that keeps nature fresh

173   *strange and self-abuse:* self-deception

174   *the initiate fear, that wants hard use:* a beginner who lacks practice

175   *young in deed:* new at crime

Question enrages him: at once, good night: 145
Stand not upon the order of your going,
But go at once.
Lennox: Good night, and better health
Attend his majesty!
Lady Macbeth: A kind good night to all! 150
      [*Exeunt all but Macbeth and Lady Macbeth*]
Macbeth: It will have blood; they say blood will have blood.
Stones have been known to move, and trees to speak;
Augures and understood relations have
By magot-pies and choughs and rooks brought forth
The secret'st man of blood. What is the night? 155
Lady Macbeth: Almost at odds with morning, which is
    which.
Macbeth: How say'st thou, that Macduff denies his person
At our great bidding?
Lady Macbeth: Did you send to him, sir? 160
Macbeth: I hear it by the way, but I will send:
There's not a one of them but in his house
I keep a servant fee'd. I will to-morrow
And betimes I will to the weird sisters:
More shall they speak, for now I am bent to know, 165
By the worst means, the worst. For mine own good
All causes shall give way; I am in blood
Stepp'd in so far, that, should I wade no more,
Returning were as tedious as go o'er:
Strange things I have in head that will to hand, 170
Which must be acted ere they may be scann'd.
Lady Macbeth: You lack the season of all natures, sleep.
Macbeth: Come, we'll to sleep. My strange and self-abuse
Is the initiate fear, that wants hard use:
We are yet but young in deed.   [*Exeunt*] 175

Act 3, Scene 4: Activities

1. Select a section of this scene for group presentation. Appoint the director and actors, and discuss the following questions before blocking and rehearsing:
   - How will the guests be seated?
   - Where will Lady Macbeth be seated?
   - How and where will the murderer appear so that he does not attract the guests' attention?
   - Will the ghost of Banquo be visible, or will he be invisible to the audience as well as the guests? If visible, how will he enter and where will he sit?
   - How will Lady Macbeth manage to calm Macbeth without the guests overhearing?
   - How will the guests behave during this time? When dismissed, how will they act?

   You may wish to make a video of your presentation.

2. As Lady Macbeth's lady-in-waiting write a letter to your friend. Describe the changes in Lady Macbeth since your last letter (see page 63) and speculate about the reasons for the changes.

3. With a partner, script either the conversation of Ross and Lennox after they leave the banquet or the conversation of two of the palace servants as they clear up the remains of the banquet. Present your dialogue to your group for their comments.

4. Your television channel has sent you to prepare a report on the banquet. As you plan the content of your report, consider the following:
   - descriptions of clothing that participants are wearing
   - the seating arrangement
   - the wording you would choose to describe the king's sudden erratic behaviour

   What other details might you include?

   Share your coverage with others.

5. If the Macbeths considered you to be a trusted friend and asked you for advice, what would you say to each to them? Write your response, taking into account what you think their future actions will be. Let them know if you feel any pity for either of them.

For the next scene . . .

Think of someone you know or have heard about who did something stupid because he or she was "over-confident." Why is confidence an advantage and over-confidence a disadvantage?

Act 3, Scene 5

In this scene . . .

On a bleak heath, we are introduced to Hecate, the queen of witches. She is angry at the three weird sisters because they have not involved her in their encounters with Macbeth. Knowing that he will seek them out next morning, however, Hecate arranges with them the details of his reception. They plan to lead Macbeth to his downfall by making him feel over-confident.

Stage direction—*Thunder:* This stage direction indicates that the actors enter through the stage trap doors.

2   *beldams:* old hags

3   *Saucy:* impudent, impertinent

7   *close contriver:* secret inventor

13   *Loves for his . . . for you:* He welcomes evil for what he may obtain, not for its own sake.

15   *Acheron:* one of the rivers of Hades, the underworld of Greek mythology. Hecate means some gloomy, hell-like place.

18   *provide:* prepare

23   *the corner:* the horn

24-25   *There hangs a vaporous drop . . . to ground:* It was believed that, given the appropriate spells, the moon would pour down a foam with magic powers.

26   *sleights:* tricks

27   *artificial sprites:* spirits or apparitions

Scene 5

A heath. Thunder.

*Enter Hecate, meeting the three
Witches.*

First Witch: Why, how now, Hecate? you look angerly.
Hecate: Have I not reason, beldams as you are,
  Saucy, and over-bold? How did you dare
  To trade and traffic with Macbeth
  In riddles and affairs of death;   5
  And I, the mistress of your charms,
  The close contriver of all harms,
  Was never call'd to bear my part,
  Or show the glory of our art?
  And, which is worse, all you have done   10
  Hath been but for a wayward son,
  Spiteful, and wrathful; who, as others do,
  Loves for his own ends, not for you.
  But make amends now: get you gone,
  And at the pit of Acheron   15
  Meet me i' the morning; thither he
  Will come to know his destiny.
  Your vessels and your spells provide,
  Your charms and everything beside.
  I am for the air; this night I'll spend   20
  Unto a dismal and a fatal end.
  Great business must be wrought ere noon:
  Upon the corner of the moon
  There hangs a vaporous drop profound;
  I'll catch it ere it come to ground: 25
  And that, distill'd by magic sleights,
  Shall raise such artificial sprites,
  As, by the strength of their illusion,

29   *confusion:* destruction

32   *security:* over-confidence, a sense of false security

35   *Sits in a foggy cloud:* This was formed by billowing drapery,
       and Hecate would be drawn into it (by pulleys) and thus disap-
       pear into the "heavens".

Shall draw him on to his confusion:
He shall spurn fate, scorn death, and bear   30
His hopes 'bove wisdom, grace, and fear:
And you all know security
Is mortals' chiefest enemy.
[*Music and a Song within, "Come away, come away," etc.*]
Hark, I am call'd; my little spirit, see,
Sits in a foggy cloud, and stays for me.   [*Exit*] 35
First Witch: Come, let's make haste: she'll soon be back
    again.   [*Exeunt*]

Act 3, Scene 5: Activity

1. Many scholars believe that this scene was not written by Shakespeare, but was added later by another poet. Discuss with your group why this scene might have been added. What aspects would make it popular with audiences? What aspects link it to the rest of the play? As the director, would you stage or omit this scene?

For the next scene . . .

Suppose you lived in an undemocratic country. How would you express your discontent with someone in authority?

Act 3, Scene 6

In this scene . . .

Lennox and another lord discuss crimes they now
are certain have been committed by Macbeth. They
also review new developments: Macbeth is furious
because Macduff refused to attend the banquet;
Malcolm is safe at the court of Edward, the King of
England; Macduff is on his way to join Malcolm and
seek England's military assistance to attack Macbeth;
and Macbeth is making preparations for defence.
Scotland, they say, is filled with fear and suffering and
they pray for a return to normality.

1   *My former speeches . . . thoughts:* What I told you before was
what you were already thinking.

3   *borne:* managed, carried out

8   *Who cannot want the thought:* who can fail to think

10   *fact:* act, deed

12   *pious:* loyal, religious; *delinquents:* criminals; *tear:* hack, butcher

13   *thralls:* slaves

19   *an't:* if it

21   *broad:* honest, blunt, unguarded

22   *tyrant:* the first such use of this word to describe Macbeth.
It means both usurper and bloodthirsty king.

24   *bestows himself:* is living

26   *due of birth:* birthright (the crown)

28   *the most pious Edward:* Edward the Confessor, who reigned
from 1042 to 1066. He was a religious king, who founded
Westminster Abbey, and was declared a saint after his death.

29-30   *the malevolence of fortune . . . high respect:* The fact that he
has lost his throne does not in any way diminish the respect with
which he is treated.

Scene 6

Forres. A room in the Palace.

Enter Lennox and another Lord.

Lennox: My former speeches have but hit your thoughts,
Which can interpret farther: only I say
Things have been strangely borne. The gracious Duncan
Was pitied of Macbeth: marry, he was dead:
And the right-valiant Banquo walk'd too late: 5
Whom, you may say, if't please you, Fleance kill'd,
For Fleance fled: men must not walk too late.
Who cannot want the thought, how monstrous
It was for Malcolm and for Donalbain
To kill their gracious father? damned fact!   10
How it did grieve Macbeth! did he not straight,
In pious rage, the two delinquents tear,
That were the slaves of drink and thralls of sleep?
Was not that nobly done? Ay, and wisely too;
For 'twould have anger'd any heart alive   15
To hear the men deny it. So that, I say,
He has borne all things well: and I do think
That, had he Duncan's sons under his key—
As, an't please heaven, he shall not—they should find
What 'twere to kill a father; so should Fleance.   20
But, peace! for from broad words, and 'cause he fail'd
His presence at the tyrant's feast, I hear,
Macduff lives in disgrace: sir, can you tell
Where he bestows himself?
Lord: The son of Duncan,   25
From whom this tyrant holds the due of birth,
Lives in the English court, and is received
Of the most pious Edward with such grace,
That the malevolence of fortune nothing
Takes from his high respect. Thither Macduff   30

31   *upon his aid:* on Malcolm's behalf

32   *Northumberland and warlike Siward:* the people of the county
of Northumberland and their earl, Siward

34   *ratify:* approve

37   *faithful:* honest, that is, to the rightful king

37   *free honours:* honours truly earned, not acquired by crime and
servility.

39   *exasperate the King:* has angered Macbeth

43   *cloudy:* sullen, surly

44   *hums:* mutters

45   *clogs:* burdens

47   *distance:* between himself and Macbeth

Is gone to pray the holy king, upon his aid
To wake Northumberland and warlike Siward:
That, by the help of these, with Him above
To ratify the work, we may again
Give to our tables meat, sleep to our nights;   35
Free from our feasts and banquets bloody knives;
Do faithful homage, and receive free honours;—
All which we pine for now: and this report
Hath so exasperate the king, that he
Prepares for some attempt of war.   40
Lennox: Sent he to Macduff?
Lord: He did: and with an absolute, "Sir, not I,"
    The cloudy messenger turns me his back,
    And hums, as who would say, "You'll rue the time
    That clogs me with this answer".   45
Lennox: And that well might
    Advise him to a caution, to hold what distance
    His wisdom can provide. Some holy angel
    Fly to the court of England and unfold
    His message ere he come, that a swift blessing   50
    May soon return to this our suffering country
    Under a hand accursed!
Lord: I'll send my prayers with him!

                                            [*Exeunt*]

Act 3, Scene 6: Activities

1. As Ross, write a letter to your relative Macduff, warning him about Macbeth. Remember that your messenger might be one of Macbeth's spies.

2. Write Lady Macbeth's diary entry for the period of time following the banquet.

Consider the Whole Act

1. If you were the illustrator of a new edition of *Macbeth*, but were requested by the publisher to provide only one illustration for Act 3, which scene, particular idea, or overall impression would you choose? Prepare a sketch, painting, or collage in colour or black and white. Display your illustration and invite classmates to discuss its effectiveness.

2. Prepare, with your group, a reader's theatre presentation of one scene, or part of a scene, from this act. When you choose your scene, keep in mind that reader's theatre depends on voices, facial expressions, and gestures for its impact. If your group wishes, you could make use of music and other sound effects. After rehearsing, present your scene to the class.

3. In your journal, write the questions you would like to ask Shakespeare or the comments you would like to make to him at this point in the play. Consider using the following beginnings as a guide:
   - Why did you . . .?
   - Why didn't you . . .?
   - I really like the way you . . .
   - I do not understand . . .
   - I do not like . . .

4. Imagine that you are a marriage counsellor. As is often the case, the Macbeths either seem unaware that they are drifting apart or are unable to do anything about it. They have not asked for your help, so all you can do is make notes as an observer. Working with a partner, write your case notes and observations.

5. A political group is forming to challenge Macbeth's rule. Create a flier that could be circulated to inform interested citizens.

For the next scene . . .

Sometimes we feel so angry or frustrated, so helpless or desperate that we lose all caution and restraint. In your journal, describe such an experience of your own or of someone you know.

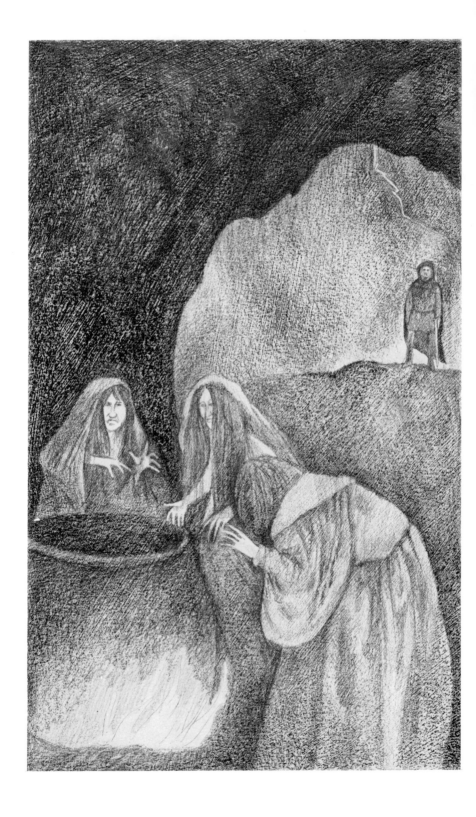

Act 4, Scene 1

In this scene . . .

The witches chant and dance around a bubbling cauldron, brewing a spell. Macbeth enters their cave, demanding that they answer his questions; in fact, he would prefer that the universe be turned to chaos rather than be denied what he wants to know. This time, the prophecies are spoken by apparitions: a head wearing a battle helmet, a blood-covered child, and a child wearing a crown and carrying a tree. They tell Macbeth to beware of Macduff; that he will not be killed by anyone born of woman; and that he will be defeated only when the trees of Birnam Wood move towards his castle. As with the earlier prophecies, his knowledge that the first is correct convinces Macbeth that the next two are also valid. His new sense of security is weakened, however, when his insistent demand about Banquo's descendants is answered by a parade of apparition-kings, each resembling Banquo.

As Macbeth curses the witches in rage, they dance and disappear. Lennox enters the cave to tell Macbeth that messengers have brought news that Macduff has fled to the English court. Furious, Macbeth swears to kill Macduff's family.

1   *brinded:* striped (perhaps Graymalkin, the first witch's familiar spirit)

2   *hedge-pig:* hedgehog

3   *Harpier:* probably the third witch's familiar spirit, a harpy, a mythological monster, half bird and half woman, who torments humans.

8   *Swelter'd venom sleeping got:* Toads' glands contain a poisonous substance and it was believed they sweated out the poison while they slept.

12   *fenny:* from a marsh

14   *newt:* lizard

16   *Adder's fork:* the forked tongue of the snake; *blind-worm's sting:* the slow-worm, a small legless lizard

23   *Witches' mummy:* a potion made from the mummified body of a witch; *maw and gulf:* the stomach and throat

24   *ravin'd:* glutted, full of food

25   *digg'd i' the dark:* poisons gathered in the dark were more potent

26   *Liver of blaspheming Jew:* The liver was believed to be the centre of passions; Jews would be seen as blasphemous because they did not believe in the divinity of Christ.

27-28   *slips of yew,/ Sliver'd in the moon's eclipse:* The yew, which often grew in graveyards, was believed to be poisonous. As eclipses were seen as catastrophes, a cutting of yew taken at this time would be especially evil and potent.

29-30   *Nose of Turk . . . strangled babe:* All these would not have been baptized, that is, admitted to the Christian church, therefore they were welcomed by witches; *Ditch-deliver'd:* born in a ditch; *drab:* prostitute

Act 4, Scene 1

A dark Cave. In the middle, a
Cauldron boiling. Thunder.

Enter the three Witches.

First Witch: Thrice the brinded cat hath mew'd.
Second Witch: Thrice; and once the hedge-pig whined.
Third Witch: Harpier cries "'Tis time, 'tis time."
First Witch: Round about the cauldron go;
   In the poison'd entrails throw.   5
   Toad, that under cold stone
   Days and nights has thirty-one
   Swelter'd venom sleeping got,
   Boil thou first i' the charmed pot!
All: Double, double, toil and trouble;   10
   Fire burn, and cauldron bubble.
Second Witch: Fillet of a fenny snake,
   In the cauldron boil and bake;
   Eye of newt, and toe of frog,
   Wool of bat, and tongue of dog,   15
   Adder's fork, and blind-worm's sting,
   Lizard's leg, and owlet's wing,
   For a charm of powerful trouble,
   Like a hell-broth boil and bubble.
All: Double, double, toil and trouble;   20
   Fire burn, and cauldron bubble.
Third Witch: Scale of dragon, tooth of wolf,
   Witches' mummy; maw and gulf
   Of the ravin'd salt-sea shark,
   Root of hemlock digg'd i' the dark,   25
   Liver of blaspheming Jew,
   Gall of goat, and slips of yew,
   Sliver'd in the moon's eclipse,
   Nose of Turk, and Tartar's lips,
   Finger of birth-strangled babe, Ditch-deliver'd by a drab,   30

31   *slab:* thick, slimy

32   *chaudron:* entrails, insides

43   *By the pricking of my thumbs:* a physical premonition of evil

50   *conjure:* demand; *that which you profess:* the black arts

51   *answer me:* Macbeth lists various disastrous events that he would prefer to have happen than not to have this question answered.

52-53   *untie the winds . . . the churches:* The winds blow so violently that they destroy churchbuildings. (It was believed that witches controlled the winds.)

53   *yesty:* foaming (like yeast)

54   *confound:* throw into confusion

55   *bladed corn be lodged:* the ripe corn be beaten down

57   *slope:* bend

59   *nature's germins:* the seeds of life, of all living things

60   *Even till destruction sicken:* until destruction sickens at its own work

66   *masters:* the evil spirits they serve

Make the gruel thick and slab;
Add thereto a tiger's chaudron,
For the ingredients of our cauldron.
All: Double, double, toil and trouble;
Fire burn, and cauldron bubble.   35
Second Witch: Cool it with a baboon's blood,
Then the charm is firm and good.
[*Enter Hecate, to the other three Witches*]
Hecate: O, well done! I commend your pains;
And every one shall share i' the gains,
And now about the cauldron sing,   40
Like elves and fairies in a ring,
Enchanting all that you put in.
        [*Music and a Song; "Black Spirits," etc. Hecate retires*]
Second Witch: By the pricking of my thumbs,
Something wicked this way comes:
Open, locks,   45
Whoever knocks.
[*Enter Macbeth*]
Macbeth: How now, you secret, black, and midnight hags!
What is't you do?
All: A deed without a name.
Macbeth: I conjure you, by that which you profess,   50
Howe'er you come to know it, answer me:
Though you untie the winds and let them fight
Against the churches; though the yesty waves
Confound and swallow navigation up;
Though bladed corn be lodged and trees blown down;   55
Though castles topple on their warders' heads;
Though palaces and pyramids do slope
Their heads to their foundations; though the treasure
Of nature's germins tumble all together,
Even till destruction sicken; answer me   60
To what I ask you.
First Witch: Speak.
Second Witch: Demand.
Third Witch: We'll answer.
First Witch: Say, if thou'dst rather hear it from our mouths,   65
Or from our masters'?
Macbeth: Call 'em, let me see 'em.

69   *her nine farrow:* her litter of nine

69-70 *grease that's sweaten/ From the murderer's gibbet:* sweat from the gallows—it was believed that one sweated grease

72   *high or low:* rank in hell

73   *office:* your function

Stage direction—*armed head:* The helmeted head probably represents that of Macbeth, cut off by Macduff.

76   *but say thou nought:* One was not permitted to speak to spirits or ghosts.

80   *harp'd:* guessed

Stage direction—*a bloody child:* This represents Macduff, and contains a clue to the meaning of "none of woman born" in the prediction that follows.

90   *take a bond of fate:* guarantee, make sure that fate comes true

91   *pale-hearted fear it lies:* I can assure my fears that they are false.

92   *thunder:* a sign of God's anger

Stage direction—*a child crowned, with a tree in his hand:* represents Malcolm and contains another clue to the prediction that follows. It suggests how Birnam wood will come to Dunsinane.

94   *issue:* offspring

First Witch: Pour in sow's blood, that hath eaten
  Her nine farrow; grease that's sweaten
  From the murderer's gibbet, throw   70
  Into the flame.
All: Come, high, or low;
  Thyself and office deftly show.
  [*Thunder. First apparition: an armed Head*]
Macbeth: Tell me, thou unknown power,—
First Witch: He knows thy thought: 75
  Hear his speech, but say thou nought.
Apparition: Macbeth! Macbeth! Macbeth! beware Macduff;
  Beware the thane of Fife. Dismiss me: enough.
                           [*Descends*]
Macbeth: Whate'er thou art, for thy good caution, thanks;
  Thou hast harp'd my fear aright: but one word more,— 80
First Witch: He will not be commanded: here's another,
  More potent than the first.
  [*Thunder. Second apparition: a bloody Child*]
Apparition: Macbeth! Macbeth! Macbeth!
Macbeth: Had I three ears, I'd hear thee.
Apparition: Be bloody, bold, and resolute; laugh to scorn 85
  The power of man, for none of woman born
  Shall harm Macbeth.   [*Descends*]
Macbeth: Then live, Macduff: what need I fear of thee?
  But yet I'll make assurance double sure.
  And take a bond of fate: thou shalt not live;   90
  That I may tell pale-hearted fear it lies,
  And sleep in spite of thunder.
  [*Thunder. Third apparition: a Child crowned, with a tree in*
    his hand]
                          What is this,
  That rises like the issue of a king,
  And wears upon his baby brow the round   95
  And top of sovereignty?
All: Listen, but speak not to't.
Apparition: Be lion-mettled, proud, and take no care
  Who chafes, who frets, or where conspirers are:
  Macbeth shall never vanquish'd be until   100
  Great Birnam wood to high Dunsinane hill
  Shall come against him.   [*Descends*]

104 *impress:* force into service

105 *bodements:* prophecies

108 *lease of nature:* length of time given by nature, the normal length of time

Stage direction—*glass:* mirror

122 *Thou art too like the spirit of Banquo:* Each of the eight kings looks like Banquo. The kings that Macbeth is shown represent the Stuart dynasty. It was believed that Fleance escaped to Wales and married a Welsh princess. Their descendant Walter returned to Scotland and became Lord Steward, founder of the Stuarts, the monarchs of Scotland. The eighth Stuart king, James VI, became James I of England in 1603. All English monarchs since then have been his descendants.

123 *sear:* scorch, burn

126 *start, eyes:* let my eyes fall from their sockets, so that I will not have to see any more

127 *the crack of doom:* the peal of thunder, to announce the Last Judgment

131 *two-fold balls and treble sceptres:* these are coronation emblems, the orb and staff. James VI of Scotland was crowned twice, at Scone and Westminster, England and became officially, King of three countries, Great Britain, France, and Ireland

133 *blood-bolter'd:* hair tangled with blood

137 *sprites:* spirits

Macbeth: That will never be:
  Who can impress the forest, bid the tree
  Unfix his earth-bound root? Sweet bodements! good!   105
  Rebellion's head, rise never, till the wood
  Of Birnam rise, and our high-placed Macbeth
  Shall live the lease of nature, pay his breath
  To time, and mortal custom. Yet my heart
  Throbs to know one thing: tell me, if your art   110
  Can tell so much: shall Banquo's issue ever
  Reign in this kingdom?
All: Seek to know no more.
Macbeth: I will be satisfied: deny me this,
  And an eternal curse fall on you! Let me know: 115
  Why sinks that cauldron? and what noise is this?

                               [*Hautboys*]

First Witch: Show!
Second Witch: Show!
Third Witch: Show!
All: Show his eyes, and grieve his heart;   120
  Come like shadows, so depart.
  [*Eight Kings appear, and pass over the Stage in order; the*
    last with a Glass in his hand; Banquo's Ghost following]
Macbeth: Thou art too like the spirit of Banquo: down!
  Thy crown does sear mine eyeballs. And thy hair,
  Thou other gold-bound brow, is like the first.
  A third is like the former. Filthy hags!   125
  Why do you show me this? A fourth? Start, eyes!
  What, will the line stretch out to the crack of doom?
  Another yet? A seventh? I'll see no more:
  And yet the eighth appears, who bears a glass
  Which shows me many more; and some I see   130
  That twofold balls and treble sceptres carry:
  Horrible sight! Now I see 'tis true;
  For the blood-bolter'd Banquo smiles upon me,
  And points at them for his. What, is this so?
First Witch: Ay, sir, all this is so: but why   135
  Stands Macbeth thus amazedly?
  Come, sisters, cheer we up his sprites,
  And show the best of our delights:
  I'll charm the air to give a sound,

140   *antic round:* strange or fantastic dance

142   *our duties did his welcome pay:* We have given him an appropriate welcome.

143   *pernicious:* destructive, fatal

144   *aye:* for ever

145   *Come in, without there:* Lennox must have been standing guard outside the witches' cavern.

151   *infected be the air whereon they ride:* a curse

158   *anticipatest:* they forestall; *dread exploits:* his plan to murder Macduff

159   *The flighty purpose . . . go with it:* Unless one acts immediately, one never carries out one's intentions.

161-162 *The very firstlings . . . of my hand:* I shall act as soon as I have an idea; I shall act on impulse.

164   *surprise:* attack suddenly

167   *That trace him in his line:* that are descended from him, or that follow in his footsteps

169   *sights:* apparitions

While you perform your antic round,   140
That this great king may kindly say
Our duties did his welcome pay.
   [*Music. The Witches dance, and vanish*]
Macbeth: Where are they? Gone? Let this pernicious hour
   Stand aye accursed in the calendar!
   Come in, without there!   145
   [*Enter Lennox*]
Lennox: What's your grace's will?
Macbeth: Saw you the weird sisters?
Lennox: No, my lord.
Macbeth: Came they not by you?
Lennox: No indeed, my lord. 150
Macbeth: Infected be the air whereon they ride,
   And damn'd all those that trust them! I did hear
   The galloping of horse: who was't came by?
Lennox: 'Tis two or three, my lord, that bring you word
   Macduff is fled to England.   155
Macbeth: Fled to England!
Lennox: Ay, my good lord.
Macbeth [*Aside*]: Time, thou anticipatest my dread exploits:
   The flighty purpose never is o'ertook
   Unless the deed go with it: from this moment,   160
   The very firstlings of my heart shall be
   The firstlings of my hand. And even now,
   To crown my thoughts with acts, be it thought and done;
   The castle of Macduff I will surprise;
   Seize upon Fife; give to the edge o' the sword   165
   His wife, his babes, and all unfortunate souls
   That trace him in his line. No boasting like a fool;
   This deed I'll do before this purpose cool:
   But no more sights!—Where are these gentlemen?
   Come, bring me where they are.   [*Exeunt*] 170

Act 4, Scene 1: Activities

1. In your group, rehearse and present a dramatic reading of the whole scene. Then do at least one of the following:

   a) Discuss the ways in which this encounter with the witches differs from that in Act 1, Scene 3.

   b) Prepare a mime of the scene up to the entrance of Lennox. Before you make your presentation, practise movements and gestures until you find those that best convey the rhythms and rituals of the scene. Present your mime to the class.

   c) Develop a chant to describe your own modern ingredients that could be added to the witches' cauldron. As a class, compare broths, to decide which is the most loathsome.

   d) Decide whether you wish to omit Hecate's lines and the songs and dances associated with her.

2. In groups, discuss Macbeth's responses to each of the prophecies in this scene. What best illustrates the fact that he ignores the contradictions of the prophecies?

3. Macbeth determines that "The very firstlings of my heart shall be / The firstlings of my hand." Describe in your journal a situation in which you or someone you know acted in this way. What were the consequences?

4. Write notes in your director's log on how you might stage the apparitions in this scene.

For the next scene . . .

If you had to choose between loyalty to your family and loyalty to your country, what decision would you make? Discuss with your group.

Act 4, Scene 2

In this scene . . .

Ross visits his relative Lady Macduff at her castle in
Fife, hoping to assure her that Macduff's flight to England was for valid reasons. She does not accept
Ross's argument, for she and her children are now
very vulnerable. After Ross leaves, Lady Macduff and
her son discuss treason and related matters and she
is amused by his intelligent and perceptive comments.
An unidentified messenger arrives to warn Lady Macduff of danger, but he comes too late. The murderers
burst in, stab the child, and pursue the screaming
Lady Macduff.

2 *patience:* self-control

9 *titles:* property, possessions

11 *wants the natural touch:* He lacks the natural human affections.

14-16 *All is the fear . . . all reason:* Such an irrational departure shows no love or wisdom, but only fear for himself.

17 *coz:* cousin

18 *school:* control

20 *The fits o' the season:* the sudden changes of these times

22 *And do not know ourselves:* and do not realize it

22-23 *when we hold rumour/ From what we fear:* when we believe rumours that are inspired by fear

27-28 *Things at the worse will cease . . . before:* The situation cannot worsen and might improve.

Scene 2

Fife. A room in Macduff's Castle.

*Enter Lady Macduff, her Son,
and Ross.*

Lady Macduff: What had he done, to make him fly the land?
Ross: You must have patience, madam.
Lady Macduff: He had none:
 His flight was madness: when our actions do not,
 Our fears do make us traitors.   5
Ross: You know not
 Whether it was his wisdom or his fear.
Lady Macduff: Wisdom! to leave his wife, to leave his babes,
 His mansion and his titles, in a place
 From whence himself does fly? He loves us not; 10
 He wants the natural touch: for the poor wren,
 The most diminutive of birds, will fight,
 Her young ones in her nest, against the owl.
 All is the fear and nothing is the love;
 As little is the wisdom, where the flight   15
 So runs against all reason.
Ross: My dearest coz,
 I pray you, school yourself; but, for your husband,
 He is noble, wise, judicious, and best knows
 The fits o' the season. I dare not speak much further: 20
 But cruel are the times, when we are traitors,
 And do not know ourselves; when we hold rumour
 From what we fear, yet know not what we fear,
 But float upon a wild and violent sea
 Each way and move. I take my leave of you: 25
 Shall not be long but I'll be here again:
 Things at the worst will cease, or else climb upward
 To what they were before. My pretty cousin,
 Blessing upon you!

32   *It would be my disgrace and your discomfort:* Ross is afraid he
     is going to cry.

34   *sirrah:* in this instance, an affectionate address to the child

40   *lime:* a sticky lime was spread on trees to catch birds

41   *pitfall:* traps; *gin:* snare

42   *poor:* small; *set for:* trapped

49   *sell again:* betray

50   *wit:* cleverness; *for thee:* for your age

56   *swears and lies:* breaks his oath

67   *poor monkey:* affectionate

Lady Macduff: Father'd he is, and yet he's fatherless.   30
Ross: I am so much a fool, should I stay longer,
   It would be my disgrace and your discomfort.
   I take my leave at once.   [*Exit Ross*]
Lady Macduff: Sirrah, your father's dead;
   And what will you do now? How will you live?   35
Son: As birds do, mother.
Lady Macduff: What, with worms and flies?
Son: With what I get, I mean; and so do they.
Lady Macduff: Poor bird! thou'dst never fear the net nor
   lime,   40
   The pitfall nor the gin.
Son: Why should I, mother? Poor birds they are not set
   for;
   My father is not dead, for all your saying.
Lady Macduff: Yes, he is dead: how wilt thou do for a   45
   father?
Son: Nay, how will you do for a husband?
Lady Macduff: Why, I can buy me twenty at any market.
Son: Then you'll buy 'em to sell again.
Lady Macduff: Thou speak'st with all thy wit, and yet, i'   50
   faith,
   With wit enough for thee.
Son: Was my father a traitor, mother?
Lady Macduff: Ay, that he was.
Son: What is a traitor?   55
Lady Macduff: Why, one that swears and lies.
Son: And be all traitors that do so?
Lady Macduff: Every one that does so is a traitor, and must
   be hanged.
Son: And must they all be hanged that swear and lie?   60
Lady Macduff: Every one.
Son: Who must hang them?
Lady Macduff: Why, the honest men.
Son: Then the liars and swearers are fools: for there are
   liars and swearers enough to beat the honest men and   65
   hang up them.
Lady Macduff: Now, God help thee, poor monkey!
   But how wilt thou do for a father?
Son: If he were dead, you'd weep for him: if you would

74   *in your state of honour I am perfect:* I am well acquainted with
      your status.

75   *doubt:* suspect, fear

76   *homely:* plain

79   *fell:* inhuman

80   *nigh:* close

85   *laudable:* commendable, praiseworthy

93   *shag-ear'd:* with shaggy hair hanging over his ears

95   *fry:* offspring

not, it were a good sign that I should quickly have a   70
  new father.
Lady Macduff: Poor prattler! how thou talk'st!
  [*Enter a Messenger*]
Messenger: Bless you, fair dame! I am not to you known,
  Though in your state of honour I am perfect.
  I doubt some danger does approach you nearly: 75
  If you will take a homely man's advice,
  Be not found here; hence, with your little ones.
  To fright you thus, methinks I am too savage;
  To do worse to you were fell cruelty,
  Which is too nigh your person. Heaven preserve you!   80
  I dare abide no longer.   [*Exit Messenger*]
Lady Macduff: Whither should I fly?
  I have done no harm. But I remember now
  I am in this earthly world, where to do harm
  Is often laudable; to do good sometime   85
  Accounted dangerous folly: why then, alas,
  Do I put up that womanly defence,
  To say, I have done no harm?—What are these faces?
  [*Enter Murderers*]
Murderer: Where is your husband?
Lady Macduff: I hope, in no place so unsanctified   90
  Where such as thou mayst find him.
Murderer: He's a traitor.
Son: Thou liest, thou shag-ear'd villain.
Murderer: What, you egg?   [*Stabbing him*]
  Young fry of treachery!   95
Son: He has kill'd me, mother:
  Run away, I pray you.   [*Dies*]
  [*Exit Lady Macduff, crying "Murder," and pursued by the
    Murderers*]

Act 4, Scene 2: Activities

1. With a partner, draw up a chart comparing the three major murders in the play. You might include such categories as victims, motivation, planning, time and place, murderers, consequences to Macbeth, and consequences to Scotland. Comment on the development you see over the course of the three murders.

2. Write a journal entry in which you record your feelings about Macduff's decision to leave his family and go to England.

3. Remembering that Scotland is now ruled by a tyrant, write a newspaper article about the murders at Fife. You may wish to invent details about Macduff's other children.

4. In your director's log,
   - Describe how you would stage the murders. Would the stabbing of both child and mother be visible and bloody? Would either or both be suggested by screams from offstage? Would either or both be partly concealed?
   - Compare your ideas for this scene with versions in films of *Macbeth* you may have seen.

For the next scene . . .

In your opinion, which qualities are essential in a political leader? Which qualities are unacceptable? Share your opinions with your group.

Act 4, Scene 3

In this scene . . .

Macduff has arrived at the court of Edward the Confessor, King of England. He meets Malcolm, and attempts to convince him that they should prepare to invade Scotland. However, Malcolm points out that he would be foolish to accept unquestioningly Macduff's appearance of loyalty. He describes in vivid detail the kind of king he would be: corrupt, greedy, lecherous, and vicious. The horrified Macduff prepares to leave, convinced that neither Scotland nor he himself can be saved. Malcolm's test has succeeded. Now able to accept Macduff's integrity, he withdraws all the accusations he has made against himself and describes the way he really is. He is virtuous, honest, loyal, and ready to serve his country. He further informs Macduff that an English force of 10,000 soldiers is ready to invade Scotland.

Malcolm praises King Edward's piety and royal virtues and describes his special ability to prophesy and to heal those afflicted with scrofula (a form of tuberculosis).

Ross arrives from Scotland and speaks of the worsening horrors of Macbeth's tyranny. Unable at first to deal with Macduff's enquiries about the safety of his family, Ross finally breaks the news of their murder. Macduff's overwhelming sorrow gradually gives way to a determination to confront and kill Macbeth.

2   *bosoms:* hearts

5   *Bestride our down-fall'n birthdom:* stand and defend our fallen native land

9   *syllable of dolour:* wail of grief

11   *redress:* set right

12   *to friend:* favourable, right

14   *sole:* mere

16   *touch'd:* injured, harmed

16-17 *something/ You may deserve of him:* You may betray me to buy yourself back into Macbeth's favour.

17   *wisdom:* it is wise

22-23 *recoil/ In an imperial charge:* give in to the pressure of a royal command

24   *transpose:* change

25   *the brightest:* Lucifer (Satan), who fell from God's grace

26   *brows of grace:* the appearance of virtue

28   *I have lost my hopes:* Macduff had expected to be warmly received by Malcolm; instead, Malcolm is suspicious of his motives.

29   *Perchance . . . doubts:* There is a connection between your disappointment and my suspicion.

Scene 3

England. Before the King's Palace.

Enter Malcolm and Macduff.

Malcolm: Let us seek out some desolate shade, and there
  Weep our sad bosoms empty.
Macduff: Let us rather
  Hold fast the mortal sword, and like good men
  Bestride our down-fall'n birthdom: each new morn   5
  New widows howl, new orphans cry, new sorrows
  Strike heaven on the face, that it resounds
  As if it felt with Scotland, and yell'd out
  Like syllable of dolour.
Malcolm: What I believe I'll wail;   10
  What know, believe; and what I can redress,
  As I shall find the time to friend, I will.
  What you have spoke, it may be so perchance.
  This tyrant, whose sole name blisters our tongues,
  Was once thought honest: you have loved him well,   15
  He hath not touch'd you yet. I am young; but something
  You may deserve of him through me; and wisdom
  To offer up a weak, poor, innocent lamb
  To appease an angry god.
Macduff: I am not treacherous.   20
Malcolm: But Macbeth is.
  A good and virtuous nature may recoil
  In an imperial charge. But I shall crave your pardon;
  That which you are, my thoughts cannot transpose;
  Angels are bright still, though the brightest fell: 25
  Though all things foul would wear the brows of grace,
  Yet grace must still look so.
Macduff: I have lost my hopes.
Malcolm: Perchance even there where I did find my doubts.

30   *rawness:* unprotected state

31   *Those precious . . . love:* Those special incentives to inspire trust and love.

33-34   *Let not . . . own safeties:* Please do not let my suspicions *(jealousies)* make you seem dishonourable. I am just protecting myself.

37-38   *Great tyranny . . . check thee:* Macduff tells tyranny (symbolized by Macbeth) to continue to prosper, as goodness (symbolized by Malcolm) will not confront it.

39   *affeer'd:* confirmed

44   *as in absolute fear:* only because I fear you

45   *yoke:* a heavy harness, a metaphor for Macbeth's tyranny

47   *withal:* also

49   *gracious England:* Edward, the King of England

50   *goodly thousands:* thousands of reliable troops

52   *wear it:* carry or display it

54   *more sundry ways:* in more ways

58   *particulars of vice so grafted:* specific kinds of evil are so strongly established

59   *open'd:* revealed

62   *confineless harms:* boundless sins

66   *I grant him:* I admit that he is

67   *luxurious:* lustful

68   *Sudden:* hasty and violent

Why in that rawness left you wife and child,   30
Those precious motives, those strong knots of love,
Without leave-taking? I pray you,
Let not my jealousies be your dishonours,
But mine own safeties. You may be rightly just,
Whatever I shall think.   35
Macduff: Bleed, bleed, poor country:
 Great tyranny, lay thou thy basis sure,
 For goodness dares not check thee: wear thou thy wrongs;
 The title is affeer'd. Fare thee well, lord:
 I would not be the villain that thou think'st   40
 For the whole space that's in the tyrant's grasp
 And the rich East to boot.
Malcolm: Be not offended:
 I speak not as in absolute fear of you.
 I think our country sinks beneath the yoke;   45
 It weeps, it bleeds, and each new day a gash
 Is added to her wounds: I think withal
 There would be hands uplifted in my right;
 And here, from gracious England, have I offer
 Of goodly thousands: but for all this,   50
 When I shall tread upon the tyrant's head,
 Or wear it on my sword, yet my poor country
 Shall have more vices than it had before,
 More suffer and more sundry ways than ever,
 By him that shall succeed.   55
Macduff: What should he be?
Malcolm: It is myself I mean: in whom I know
 All the particulars of vice so grafted,
 That, when they shall be open'd, black Macbeth
 Will seem as pure as snow, and the poor state 60
 Esteem him as a lamb, being compared.
 With my confineless harms.
Macduff: Not in the legions
 Of horrid hell can come a devil more damn'd
 In evils to top Macbeth.   65
Malcolm: I grant him bloody,
 Luxurious, avaricious, false, deceitful,
 Sudden, malicious, smacking of every sin
 That has a name; but there's no bottom, none,

70   *voluptuousness:* lechery or lustfulness

72   *cistern:* a water tank that needs constantly to be refilled

73   *continent impediments:* restraints; *o'erbear:* overcome

74   *will:* lustful desires

76-77   *Boundless intemperance . . . tyranny:* The inability to control one's instincts is like being a slave to nature.

78   *untimely emptying:* the premature loss of the throne

81   *Convey:* secretly take

83   *there cannot be . . . so inclin'd:* You cannot desire as many women as will make themselves available to a king.

88   *ill-composed affection:* evil character

89   *staunchless avarice:* insatiable greed

90   *cut off:* dispossess

92-93   *my more having . . . hunger more:* The more I obtained, the more I would want.

93   *forge:* create, invent

97   *pernicious:* dangerous, deadly

98   *summer-seeming:* youthful

99   *sword:* ruin, destruction

100   *foisons:* plenty, bounteous harvests of wealth

101   *of your mere own:* even just from your own royal property; *portable:* bearable

102   *weigh'd:* counterbalanced

103   *king-becoming graces:* the virtues that are appropriate for a king

104   *verity:* truthfulness; *temperance:* self-control

105   *Bounty:* generosity; *lowliness:* humility

108   *division:* variation; *several;* separate

In my voluptousness: your wives, your daughters,   70
Your matrons, and your maids, could not fill up
The cistern of my lust: and my desire
All continent impediments would o'erbear,
That did oppose my will: better Macbeth
Than such an one to reign.   75
Macduff: Boundless intemperance
In nature is a tyranny; it hath been
Th' untimely emptying of the happy throne,
And fall of many kings. But fear not yet
To take upon you what is yours: you may   80
Convey your pleasures in a spacious plenty,
And yet seem cold, the time you may so hoodwink:
We have willing dames enough; there cannot be
That vulture in you, to devour so many
As will to greatness dedicate themselves,   85
Finding it so inclined.
Malcolm: With this there grows,
In my most ill-compos'd affection, such
A stanchless avarice, that, were I King,
I should cut off the nobles for their lands,   90
Desire his jewels, and this other's house:
And my more-having would be as a sauce
To make me hunger more, that I should forge
Quarrels unjust against the good and loyal,
Destroying them for wealth.   95
Macduff: This avarice
Sticks deeper, grows with more pernicious root
Than summer-seeming lust, and it hath been
The sword of our slain kings: yet do not fear;
Scotland hath foisons to fill up your will   100
Of your mere own: all these are portable,
With other graces weigh'd.
Malcolm: But I have none: the king-becoming graces,
As justice, verity, temperance, stableness,
Bounty, perseverance, mercy, lowliness,   105
Devotion, patience, courage, fortitude,
I have no relish of them, but abound
In the division of each several crime,
Acting it many ways. Nay, had I power, I should

110   *concord:* harmony, agreement

111   *Uproar:* throw into confusion; *confound:* destroy

118   *untitled:* without hereditary rights to the throne, illegal

119   *wholesome:* healthy

120   *the truest issue:* the rightful heir

121   *interdiction:* condemnation

122   *does blaspheme his breed:* dishonours his forebears

125   *Died:* through her religious observances prepared for death

126   *repeat'st:* blame, accuse

127   *Have banished me:* Macduff means either that these same sins in Macbeth have forced him into exile, or that, because Malcolm has dashed his hopes too, he will never be able to go back; *breast:* heart

129-132   *Macduff, this noble . . . and honour:* Macduff's display of feeling, the product of honesty and true love of country, has convinced Malcolm of his trustworthiness and integrity.

133   *trains:* tricks, plots

134   *modest wisdom:* ordinary caution

137   *I put myself to thy direction:* I am ready to carry out your plans

138   *Unspeak:* withdraw; *detraction:* accusations; *abjure:* renounce

141   Unknown to woman: pure, chaste; *was forsworn:* lied

146   *this upon myself:* these lies about myself

148   *here-approach:* coming here

Pour the sweet milk of concord into hell,   110
Uproar the universal peace, confound
All unity on earth.
Macduff: O Scotland, Scotland!
Malcolm: If such a one be fit to govern, speak:
I am as I have spoken.   115
Macduff: Fit to govern!
No, not to live. O nation miserable!
With an untitled tyrant bloody-sceptred,
When shalt thou see thy wholesome days again,
Since that the truest issue of thy throne   120
By his own interdiction stands accursed,
And does blaspheme his breed? Thy royal father
Was a most sainted king: the queen that bore thee,
Oftener upon her knees than on her feet,
Died every day she lived. Fare thee well!   125
These evils thou repeat'st upon thyself
Have banished me from Scotland. O my breast,
Thy hope ends here!
Malcolm: Macduff, this noble passion,
Child of integrity, hath from my soul   130
Wiped the black scruples, reconciled my thoughts
To thy good truth and honour. Devilish Macbeth
By many of these trains hath sought to win me
Into his power; and modest wisdom plucks me
From over-credulous haste: but God above   135
Deal between thee and me! for even now
I put myself to thy direction, and
Unspeak mine own detraction; here abjure
The taints and blames I laid upon myself,
For strangers to my nature. I am yet   140
Unknown to woman; never was forsworn;
Scarcely have coveted what was mine own,
At no time broke my faith, would not betray
The devil to his fellow, and delight
No less in truth, than life: my first false speaking   145
Was this upon myself: what I am truly,
Is thine and my poor country's to command:
Whither indeed, before thy here-approach,
Old Siward, with ten thousand warlike men,

150   *Already at a point:* ready, fully equipped

151-152 *and the chance of goodness/ Be like our warranted quarrel:* May our chance of success be equal to the justness of our cause.

155   *anon:* soon

158   *That stay his cure:* that wait for him to cure them

158-159 *their malady convinces/ The great assay of art:* Their disease cannot be cured by the doctors' skills.

161   *presently amend:* immediately recover

164   *the evil:* scrofula, a tuberculous swelling of the lymph glands in the neck. It was believed that King Edward and his successors could cure the disease by touching the patient.

168   *strangely-visited:* afflicted in a strange manner

170   *mere:* utter

171   *stamp:* coin

172   *'tis spoken:* people say

173   *he leaves:* he hands down to his successors

174   *benediction:* sacred power to heal

177   *speak:* proclaim, show him to be

179   *My countryman:* Ross is wearing distinctively Scottish clothing.

182   *means:* circumstances

Already at a point, was setting forth. 150
Now we'll together, and the chance of goodness
Be like our warranted quarrel! Why are you silent?
Macduff: Such welcome and unwelcome things at once
    'Tis hard to reconcile.
[*Enter a Doctor*]
Malcolm: Well, more anon. Comes the king forth, I pray 155
    you?
Doctor: Ay, sir: there are a crew of wretched souls
    That stay his cure: their malady convinces
    The great assay of art; but at his touch,
    Such sanctity hath heaven given his hand, 160
    They presently amend.
Malcolm: I thank you, doctor. [*Exit Doctor*]
Macduff: What's the disease he means?
Malcolm: 'Tis call'd the evil:
    A most miraculous work in this good king: 165
    Which often, since my here-remain in England,
    I have seen him do. How he solicits heaven,
    Himself best knows: but strangely-visited people,
    All swoln and ulcerous, pitiful to the eye,
    The mere despair of surgery, he cures, 170
    Hanging a golden stamp about their necks,
    Put on with holy prayers: and 'tis spoken,
    To the succeeding royalty he leaves
    The healing benediction. With this strange virtue
    He hath a heavenly gift of prophecy, 175
    And sundry blessings hang about his throne
    That speak him full of grace.
[*Enter Ross*]
Macduff: See, who comes here?
Malcolm: My countryman; but yet I know him not.
Macduff: My ever-gentle cousin, welcome hither. 180
Malcolm: I know him now: good God, betimes remove
    The means that makes us strangers!
Ross: Sir, amen.
Macduff: Stands Scotland where it did?
Ross: Alas, poor country, 185
    Almost afraid to know itself! It cannot
    Be call'd our mother, but our grave: where nothing,

188 *But who knows nothing:* only someone who does not know what is going on

190 *not mark'd:* nothing special, not noticed

191 *A modern ecstasy:* a commonplace emotion

194 *or ere they sicken:* before they ever fall ill

196 *nice:* exact

198 *That of an hour's age doth hiss the speaker:* Anything that happened more than an hour ago is old news (and the person telling it is hissed at because it is out of date).

199 *teems:* produces

206 *a niggard:* mean, stingy

209 *out:* in arms, rebelling (against Macbeth)

210 *Which was to my belief witness'd the rather:* I believe there was evidence to support the rumour.

212 *your eye in Scotland:* your appearance. Ross is speaking to Malcolm.

214 *doff:* get rid of, remove

219 *gives out:* proclaims. Siward is said to be the most experienced and the best soldier in the Christian world.

220 *would:* I wish

223 *latch:* catch

225 *fee-grief:* a grief concerning only one person (from a legal term that indicates private ownership of land)

But who knows nothing, is once seen to smile;
Where sighs and groans and shrieks that rend the air,
Are made not mark'd; where violent sorrow seems   190
A modern ecstasy; the dead man's knell
Is there scarce ask'd for who; and good men's lives
Expire before the flowers in their caps,
Dying or ere they sicken.
Macduff: O, relation   195
Too nice, and yet too true!
Malcolm: What's the newest grief?
Ross: That of an hour's age doth hiss the speaker;
Each minute teems a new one.
Macduff: How does my wife?   200
Ross: Why, well.
Macduff: And all my children?
Ross: Well too.
Macduff: The tyrant has not batter'd at their peace?
Ross: No; they were well at peace when I did leave them.   205
Macduff: Be not a niggard of your speech: how goes it?
Ross: When I came hither to transport the tidings,
Which I have heavily borne, there ran a rumour
Of many worthy fellows that were out;
Which was to my belief, witness'd the rather,   210
For that I saw the tyrant's power a-foot:
Now is the time of help; your eye in Scotland
Would create soldiers, make our women fight
To doff their dire distresses.
Malcolm: Be't their comfort   215
We are coming thither: gracious England hath
Lent us good Siward and ten thousand men;
An older and a better soldier none
That Christendom gives out.
Ross: Would I could answer 220
This comfort with the like! But I have words
That would be howl'd out in the desert air,
Where hearing should not latch them.
Macduff: What concern they?
The general cause? or is it a fee-grief,   225
Due to some single breast?
Ross: No mind that's honest

229   *Pertains:* belongs

233   *possess them with:* inform them of

236   *surpris'd:* suddenly attacked

238   *quarry:* hunted animals. Ross puns on deer and dear.

241   *ne'er pull your hat upon your brows:* Macduff, unable to speak, tries to hide his face.

243   *o'er-fraught:* over-burdened

251-252 *Let's make medicines . . . deadly grief:* As one passion drives out another, Malcolm suggests that the best way for Macduff to cure his grief is to put revenge in its place.

253   *He has no children:* It is not clear to whom "he" refers. Macduff may mean Malcolm, thus suggesting that Malcolm cannot understand his grief. Alternatively, Macduff may mean Macbeth, suggesting that the tyrant is able to murder children, because he has never experienced paternal love. Macduff may also mean that, as Macbeth has no children, he cannot take appropriate revenge.

254   *hell-kite:* a bird of prey that swoops on its quarry

255   *dam:* mother

257   *Dispute:* fight against it

262-265 *Sinful Macduff . . . on their souls:* Macduff, seeing himself as sinful and worthless, (*naught*) believes that it was his own wickedness (*demerits*) that caused heaven not to intervene and prevent the slaughter.

266   *whetstone:* a stone on which a blade can be sharpened

But in it shares some woe, though the main part
Pertains to you alone.
Macduff: If it be mine,   230
Keep it not from me, quickly let me have it.
Ross: Let not your ears despise my tongue for ever,
Which shall possess them with the heaviest sound
That ever yet they heard.
Macduff: Hum! I guess at it.   235
Ross: Your castle is surprised; your wife, and babes
Savagely slaughter'd: to relate the manner,
Were, on the quarry of these murder'd deer,
To add the death of you.
Malcolm: Merciful heaven!   240
What, man! ne'er pull your hat upon your brows;
Give sorrow words: the grief that does not speak
Whispers the o'er-fraught heart, and bids it break.
Macduff: My children too?
Ross: Wife, children, servants, all   245
That could be found.
Macduff: And I must be from thence!
My wife kill'd too?
Ross: I have said.
Malcolm: Be comforted: 250
Let's make us medicines of our great revenge,
To cure this deadly grief.
Macduff: He has no children. All my pretty ones?
Did you say all? O, hell-kite! All?
What, all my pretty chickens and their dam   255
At one fell swoop?
Malcolm: Dispute it like a man.
Macduff: I shall do so;
But I must also feel it as a man:
I cannot but remember such things were,   260
That were most precious to me. Did heaven look on,
And would not take their part? Sinful Macduff,
They were all struck for thee! naught that I am,
Not for their own demerits, but for mine,
Fell slaughter on their souls: heaven rest them now.   265
Malcolm: Be this the whetstone of your sword: let grief
Convert to anger; blunt not the heart, enrage it.

268   *play the woman . . . eyes:* cry

269   *braggart with my tongue:* boast

270   *intermission:* delay; *front to front:* face to face

272-273 *if he 'scape/ Heaven forgive him too:* If he escapes (from my sword) it will be a sign that both heaven and I forgive him. That is, Macduff believes that none of this will happen.

275   *power:* army

276   *Our lack is nothing but our leave:* We have only to take leave of the king

276-277 *Macbeth is ripe for shaking:* The time is perfect (the metaphor suggests that this is the exact time when the ripe fruit is ready to fall from the tree).

277-278 *the powers above/ Put on their instruments:* The forces of good arm themselves; that is, are ready to assist.

279   *The night is long . . . day:* dawn (the symbol of good) will soon break to displace night (the symbol of evil).

Macduff: O, I could play the woman with mine eyes,
    And braggart with my tongue! But, gentle heavens,
    Cut short all intermission; front to front,   270
    Bring thou this fiend of Scotland and myself;
    Within my sword's length set him; if he 'scape,
    Heaven forgive him too!
Malcolm: This tune goes manly.
    Come, go we to the king; our power is ready;   275
    Our lack is nothing but our leave. Macbeth
    Is ripe for shaking, and the powers above
    Put on their instruments. Receive what cheer you may;
    The night is long that never finds the day.
                                 [Exeunt]

Act 4, Scene 3: Activities

1. Assume you are a Scottish noble who has accompanied Macduff to Scotland. Write a diary entry in which you assess what sort of king Malcolm will be, especially in comparison with Duncan and Macbeth.

2. Could *Macbeth* be made into a movie about good and evil? Could Malcolm and Macduff be the "good guys" and Macbeth be the "bad guy"? What characteristics would qualify or disqualify them? Share your ideas with your group.

3. With a partner, list the admirable qualities of King Edward. Next to each, write a matching or opposite characteristic for Macbeth.

4. How might you tell some very upsetting news to a friend? How does Ross handle this mission? In your journal, explain how you would have broken the news to Macduff.

5. Modern directors often omit part or all of this scene. Decide with your group whether you would cut or drop it. What would you gain and lose as a result?

Act 4: Consider the Whole Act

1. Do you agree with Macduff's description of Macbeth as "this fiend of Scotland," or do you have some sympathy left for Macbeth? Share your ideas with your group.

2. As one of the spies Macbeth has sent to England, it is your job to report Macduff and Malcolm's invasion plans. With a partner, role-play the conversation you have with Macbeth on your return to Scotland.

3. As Malcolm, write a letter to Donalbain telling him how you feel on the eve of your departure to Scotland.

4. Imagine that, as Malcolm bids farewell to King Edward, the king uses his powers of prophecy to foretell Malcolm's future. Write the prophecy.

5. With your group, identify the characters in this act who seek revenge. Draw up a chart to show what factors motivate each of them and what effect each one might have on the outcome of the play.

For the next scene . . .

What kind of behaviour have you observed in children who are trying to conceal guilt? How do you conceal your guilty conscience?

Act 5, Scene 1

In this scene . . .

The Macbeths are now living at Dunsinane Castle,
probably because it is on a hill which makes it easier
to fortify and defend. A doctor has been employed
to watch over Lady Macbeth. The queen's lady-in-
waiting is worried about her mistress' behaviour. She
has seen her sleepwalking, always with a candle and
often appearing to be washing her hands. She also
writes on a piece of paper which she then locks
away. Lady Macbeth also talks in her sleep but the
lady-in-waiting, concerned for her own safety, refuses
to repeat what she has heard. Instead, she has asked
the doctor to wait up at night with her and observe Lady
Macbeth's behaviour for himself. As they watch, the
queen enters, her speech a jumbled but vivid recreation
of the murders. She is obsessed with the impossibility
of cleansing her hands of the blood she still sees and
smells. The doctor realizes that he cannot cure such
deep mental disturbance, and warns the lady-in-waiting
to watch Lady Macbeth closely, for he suspects she
is suicidal.

Stage direction—*Dunsinane:* a fortified castle on Dunsinane Hill. (See map, page 4.) *Doctor of Physic:* a physician

3   *went into the field:* started preparing for battle

4   *nightgown:* dressing gown

5   *closet:* place where valuables were kept; chest

8   *a great perturbation in nature:* a serious disturbance in her nature

9   *watching:* staying awake

10   *slumbery agitation:* activities in her sleep

14   *meet:* suitable

Stage direction—*taper:* thin candle

17   *this is her very guise:* this is the way she has done it before

18   *stand close:* hide yourself

23   *sense is shut:* do not see

Act 5, Scene 1

Dunsinane. A room in the Castle.

Enter a Doctor of Physic, and a waiting Gentlewoman.

Doctor: I have two nights watched with you, but can perceive no truth in your report. When was it she last walked?

Gentlewoman: Since his majesty went into the field, I have seen her rise from her bed, throw her nightgown upon her, unlock her closet, take forth paper, fold it, write 5 upon't, read it, afterwards seal it, and again return to bed; yet all this while in a most fast sleep.

Doctor: A great perturbation in nature, to receive at once the benefit of sleep and do the effects of watching! In this slumbery agitation, besides her walking and other 10 actual performances, what, at any time, have you heard her say?

Gentlewoman: That, sir, which I will not report after her.

Doctor: You may to me, and 'tis most meet you should.

Gentlewoman: Neither to you nor any one, having no witness 15 to confirm my speech.

[*Enter Lady Macbeth, with a taper*]

Lo you, here she comes! This is her very guise; and, upon my life, fast asleep. Observe her: stand close.

Doctor: How came she by that light?

Gentlewoman: Why, it stood by her: she has light by her 20 continually; 'tis her command.

Doctor: You see, her eyes are open.

Gentlewoman: Ay, but their sense is shut.

Doctor: What is it she does now? Look, how she rubs her hands. 25

29 *yet:* still, even after all this washing

31 *satisfy:* support

32 *One; two:* perhaps the clock striking was to signal that the time was right for Duncan's murder

35 *when none can call our power to account:* Lady Macbeth refers to the belief that "The King can do no wrong." In other words, the monarch was above the law.

42 *starting:* jumpiness

43 *Go to, go to:* a reproach or rebuke to Lady Macbeth

49 *sorely charged:* heavily burdened

51 *dignity:* value; all that the queen possesses

54 *This disease is beyond my practice:* I am not able to treat this malady. (The treatment of mental illness is comparatively modern.)

59 *on's:* of his

60 *Even so:* her words indicate to the doctor another reason for her guilt

Gentlewoman: It is an accustomed action with her, to seem
  thus washing her hands: I have known her continue
  in this a quarter of an hour.
Lady Macbeth: Yet here's a spot.
Doctor: Hark! she speaks: I will set down what comes from   30
  her, to satisfy my remembrance the more strongly.
Lady Macbeth: Out, damned spot! out, I say! One; two: why,
  then 'tis time to do't. Hell is murky. Fie, my lord,
  fie! a soldier and afeard? What need we fear who knows
  it, when none can call our power to account? Yet who   35
  would have thought the old man to have had so much
  blood in him!
Doctor: Do you mark that?
Lady Macbeth: The thane of Fife had a wife, where is she
  now? What, will these hands ne'er be clean? No more   40
  o'that, my lord, no more o'that: you mar all with this
  starting.
Doctor: Go to, go to; you have known what you should not.
Gentlewoman: She has spoke what she should not, I am sure
  of that: heaven knows what she has known.   45
Lady Macbeth: Here's the smell of blood still: all the
  perfumes of Arabia will not sweeten this little hand.
  Oh, oh, oh!
Doctor: What a sigh is there! The heart is sorely charged.
Gentlewoman: I would not have such a heart in my bosom,   50
  for the dignity of the whole body.
Doctor: Well, well, well,—
Gentlewoman: Pray God it be, sir.
Doctor: This disease is beyond my practice: yet I have known
  those which have walked in their sleep who have died   55
  holily in their beds.
Lady Macbeth: Wash your hands, put on your nightgown;
  look not so pale: I tell you yet again, Banquo's buried;
  he cannot come out on's grave.
Doctor: Even so?   60
Lady Macbeth: To bed, to bed; there's knocking at the gate;
  come, come, come, come, give me your hand: what's
  done cannot be undone; to bed, to bed, to bed.
                              [*Exit Lady Macbeth*]
Doctor: Will she go now to bed?

66   *Foul whisperings are abroad:* ugly rumours are circulating

68   *discharge:* confide

69   *divine:* priest or clergyman

71   *means of all annoyance:* anything she could use to harm herself

73   *mated:* astonished

Gentlewoman: Directly.   65
Doctor: Foul whisperings are abroad: unnatural deeds
   Do breed unnatural troubles: infected minds
   To their deaf pillows will discharge their secrets:
   More needs she the divine than the physician.
   God, God forgive us all! Look after her;   70
   Remove from her the means of all annoyance,
   And still keep eyes upon her. So good night:
   My mind she has mated, and amazed my sight:
   I think, but dare not speak.
Gentlewoman: Good night, good doctor.   75
                               [*Exeunt*]

Act 5, Scene 1: Activities

1. As an illustrator, what aspect of this scene would you emphasize? Draw a sketch or describe your illustration in words. How does your idea compare with the illustration on page 208?

2. With a partner, identify which specific actions and speeches Lady Macbeth refers to in this scene. Do you feel sympathy for Lady Macbeth? Explain your response.

3. a) If you were an actress, would you wish to play Lady Macbeth? Why or why not?

   b) If you were a casting director, which actress would you choose to play the part of Lady Macbeth? Why?

   Share your ideas with your group.

4. The doctor claims that Lady Macbeth's illness is "beyond my practice". However, he may simply be protecting himself. Write the report he will keep for his private records.

5. As Lady Macbeth's lady-in-waiting, write to your friend describing the changes in your mistress since you last wrote. You might like to warn your friend that your information is confidential.

6. Write the secret document that Lady Macbeth has written in her sleep and locked in her closet.

For the next scenes . . .

Have you ever felt that everyone you know has turned against you? What were the circumstances? How did you deal with the situation?

Act 5, Scenes 2 and 3

In these scenes . . .

The Scottish nobles Menteith, Caithness, Angus, and Lennox are on their way to Birnam Wood near Dunsinane to join with the English forces and their leaders, Malcolm, Macduff, and Siward. All are prepared to die for their country and for the restoration of order.

Macbeth, awaiting attack in the fortified castle at Dunsinane, has been deserted by everyone except his employees who are forced to remain. He receives the news that the English forces have been sighted. As he prepares for combat, he reflects on the emptiness of his present and future life. The doctor reports that nothing can be done to help Lady Macbeth; Macbeth sees a parallel between her illness and Scotland's condition. He reassures himself by repeating the prophecies that he will not be defeated until Birnam Wood moves to Dunsinane and that he cannot be killed by anyone born of a woman.

Stage direction—*colours:* flags

3   *dear causes:* heartfelt, sincere

4-5   *Would to the bleeding and grim alarm / Excite the mortified man:* would arouse even a dead man to the call to arms

9   *file:* list

11   *unrough:* smooth-faced, beardless

12   *Protest their first of manhood:* proclaim that they are now men

17-18 *He cannot buckle . . . rule:* The kingdom is rebellious and he can no longer control it. The metaphor suggests that the diseased (*distemper'd*) body is so far advanced in illness that it cannot even tolerate the control of a belt (*buckle . . . within the belt of rule.*)

21   *minutely:* every minute; *upbraid:* scold, punish; *his faith-breach:* his own treason

22-23 *move only in command . . . love:* obey him only because they have to, not at all for love of him

23-25 *now does he feel . . . thief:* he now seems a small and evil man, a travesty of a king. The metaphor indicates clothing that is not his own.

27   *His pester'd senses:* his tormented nerves; *to recoil and start:* if they are jumpy

Scene 2

The country near Dunsinane.

Enter, with drums and colours,
Menteith, Caithness, Angus,
Lennox, and Soldiers.

Menteith: The English power is near, led on by Malcolm,
  His uncle Siward and the good Macduff.
  Revenges burn in them: for their dear causes
  Would to the bleeding and the grim alarm
  Excite the mortified man.   5
Angus: Near Birnam wood
  Shall we well meet them; that way are they coming.
Caithness: Who knows if Donalbain be with his brother?
Lennox: For certain, sir, he is not: I have a file
  Of all the gentry: there is Siward's son,   10
  And many unrough youths, that even now
  Protest their first of manhood.
Menteith: What does the tyrant?
Caithness: Great Dunsinane he strongly fortifies:
  Some say he's mad; others, that lesser hate him,   15
  Do call it valiant fury: but, for certain,
  He cannot buckle his distemper'd cause
  Within the belt of rule.
Angus: Now does he feel
  His secret murders sticking on his hands;   20
  Now minutely revolts upbraid his faith-breach;
  Those he commands move only in command,
  Nothing in love: now does he feel his title
  Hang loose about him, like a giant's robe
  Upon a dwarfish thief.   25
Menteith: Who then shall blame
  His pester'd senses to recoil, and start,
  When all that is within him does condemn
  Itself for being there?

32   *medicine:* Malcolm; *weal:* land

33   *purge:* cleansing, cure. Caithness refers to the belief that a fever could be cured by drawing blood out of the patient.

36   *dew:* water; *sovereign flower:* true king's cause; *drown the weeds:* destroy the evil

Caithness: Well, march we on,   30
  To give obedience where 'tis truly owed:
  Meet we the medicine of the sickly weal,
  And with him pour we, in our country's purge,
  Each drop of us.
Lennox: Or so much as it needs,   35
  To dew the sovereign flower, and drown the weeds,
  Make we our march towards Birnam.

                             [Exeunt, marching]

1   *let them fly all:* let all the thanes defect to Malcolm

3   *taint:* weaken

5   *All mortal consequences:* all things to do with human affairs

8   *the English epicures:* The English were reputed to live in greater comfort than the hardy Scots.

9   *I sway by:* that directs my actions

11   *The devil damn thee black:* it was believed a damned soul turned black; *loon:* fool

12   *goose look:* look of cowardice

16   *over-red thy fear:* cover your fearful white face with blood

17   *lily-livered:* It was believed that the liver was the source of courage, so a coward would have a white liver; *patch:* fool, clown.

18   *linen:* bleached or white

19   *counsellors to fear:* encourage others to fear also; *whey:* the part of the milk that remains liquid when the rest turns to curds

22   *Seyton:* Macbeth's armour bearer

23   *push:* attack

24   *Will cheer me ever, or dis-seat me now:* will either make me safe or dethrone me. Macbeth plays on the words "cheer," meaning comfort, and "chair," meaning keep seated or enthroned.

25   *way of life:* course of my life

26   *sear:* dry, withered

30   *mouth-honour:* lip-service, flattery

31   *fain:* willingly

Scene 3

Dunsinane. A room in the Castle.

*Enter Macbeth, Doctor, and
Attendants.*

Macbeth: Bring me no more reports; let them fly all;
  Till Birnam wood remove to Dunsinane
  I cannot taint with fear. What's the boy Malcolm?
  Was he not born of woman? The spirits that know
  All mortal consequences have pronounced me thus: 5
  "Fear not, Macbeth; no man that's born of woman
  Shall e'er have power upon thee". Then fly, false thanes,
  And mingle with the English epicures:
  The mind I sway by and the heart I bear
  Shall never sag with doubt nor shake with fear.   10
  [*Enter a Servant*]
  The devil damn thee black, thou cream-faced loon!
  Where gott'st thou that goose look?
Servant: There is ten thousand——
Macbeth: Geese, villain?
Servant: Soldiers, sir.   15
Macbeth: Go, prick thy face, and over-red thy fear,
  Thou lily-liver'd boy. What soldiers, patch?
  Death of thy soul! those linen cheeks of thine
  Are counsellors to fear. What soldiers, whey-face?
Servant: The English force, so please you.   20
Macbeth: Take thy face hence.   [*Exit Servant*]
                 Seyton! I am sick at heart,
  When I behold—Seyton, I say!—This push
  Will cheer me ever, or dis-seat me now.
  I have lived long enough: my way of life   25
  Is fallen into the sear, the yellow leaf,
  And that which should accompany old age,
  As honour, love, obedience, troops of friends,
  I must not look to have; but, in their stead,
  Curses, not loud but deep, mouth-honour, breath,   30
  Which the poor heart would fain deny, and dare not.
  Seyton!

40   *moe:* more; *skirr:* scour

44   *thick-coming fancies:* hallucinations that crowd in on each other

47   *minister:* treat

49   *Raze:* erase; *written:* permanent

50   *oblivious antidote:* a medication to cause forgetfulness

51   *stuff'd:* choked, overburdened

55   *physic:* medical science

56   *staff:* baton of command

58   *dispatch:* hurry

58-59 *cast/The water of my land:* analyze the urine

60   *pristine:* perfect

62   *Pull't off:* Seyton has been helping Macbeth to put on his armour; now Macbeth tells Seyton to remove one piece.

63   *rhubarb, senna, or what purgative drug:* What preparation would cleanse Scotland of the English?

67   *Bring it:* the item of armour taken off by Seyton

68   *bane:* ruin

[*Enter Seyton*]
Seyton: What's your gracious pleasure?
Macbeth: What news more?
Seyton: All is confirm'd, my lord, which was reported.   35
Macbeth: I'll fight, till from my bones my flesh be hack'd.
  Give me my armour.
Seyton: 'Tis not needed yet.
Macbeth: I'll put it on.
  Send out moe horses, skirr the country round;   40
  Hang those that talk of fear. Give me mine armour.
  How does your patient, doctor?
Doctor: Not so sick, my lord,
  As she is troubled with thick-coming fancies,
  That keep her from her rest.   45
Macbeth: Cure her of that.
  Canst thou not minister to a mind diseased,
  Pluck from the memory a rooted sorrow,
  Raze out the written troubles of the brain,
  And with some sweet oblivious antidote   50
  Cleanse the stuff'd bosom of that perilous stuff
  Which weighs upon the heart?
Doctor: Therein the patient
  Must minister to himself.
Macbeth: Throw physic to the dogs, I'll none of it.   55
  Come, put mine armour on; give me my staff.
  Seyton, send out. Doctor, the thanes fly from me.
  Come, sir, dispatch. If thou couldst, doctor, cast
  The water of my land, find her disease
  And purge it to a sound and pristine health,   60
  I would applaud thee to the very echo,
  That should applaud again. Pull't off, I say.
  What rhubarb, senna, or what purgative drug,
  Would scour these English hence? Hearest thou of them?
Doctor: Ay, my good lord; your royal preparation   65
  Makes us hear something.
Macbeth: Bring it after me.
  I will not be afraid of death and bane,
  Til Birnam forest come to Dunsinane.   [*Exit*]
Doctor [Aside]: Were I from Dunsinane away and clear,   70
  Profit again should hardly draw me here.

Act 5, Scenes 2 and 3: Activities

1. If you were a Scottish soldier, would you desert Macbeth? Why or why not? Share your ideas with your group.

2. With a partner, script the conversation between two Scots, one of whom has joined Malcolm's forces and is trying to persuade the other to do the same.

3. What do you hope to have in your old age? What does Macbeth want? What does he see in his future instead? What would you do if you were in his situation? Write your responses in your notebook.

4. Write either the doctor's private report after his observation of Macbeth's behaviour or the soliloquy of Seyton if he were to remain on the stage a few minutes after the exit of Macbeth and the doctor. Present it to your group for their comments.

5. As a director, how would you emphasize the contrasts between scenes 2 and 3? Make notes in your director's log on staging directions such as lighting, scenery, and action.

For the next scenes . . .

Describe a situation in which you felt trapped. How did you behave?

Act 5, Scenes 4, 5, and 6

In these scenes . . .

The Scottish forces have joined the English army at Birnam Wood. Malcolm, as commander, orders each soldier to cut down and carry a branch. This ploy will prevent Macbeth's scouts from accurately assessing the numbers of soldiers in Malcolm's army as it marches to Dunsinane.

Macbeth, in the meantime, is confident that Dunsinane Castle can resist any siege, regretting only that he does not have enough soldiers left to charge against Malcolm's army. As he ponders that he is so accustomed to living with horror that he no longer experiences fear, he is told that Lady Macbeth is dead. Life seems to him now futile and empty. A messenger arrives to report, in disbelief, that Birnam Wood is moving towards the castle. At last, Macbeth realizes that he has been deceived. Believing that he cannot win, whether he stays in the castle or attacks, Macbeth decides that he will die fighting and calls his troops to arms – and thereby makes it possible for Malcolm to capture Dunsinane.

Upon their arrival at Dunsinane, Malcolm orders his soldiers to throw down their camouflage of branches and to proceed to battle.

2   *chambers:* bedrooms

3   *We doubt it nothing:* we do not doubt it at all

7   *shadow:* hide, obscure

8   *host:* army

8-9   *make discovery/Err:* prevent Macbeth's scouts from reporting accurately on our numbers

12-13   *will endure/Our setting down before't:* will allow us to lay siege to it

15   *advantage to be gone:* chance to escape

16   *Both more and less:* high and low ranks

17   *constrained things:* those who have been forced

19-20   *Let our just censures/ Attend the true event:* Macduff warns against too much optimism.

24   *When we shall say . . . owe:* the difference between what we say we have and what we actually have won

26   *certain issue strokes must arbitrate:* Only actual fighting can decide these things.

Scene 4

Country near Birnam Wood.

*Enter, with drum and colours,
Malcolm, old Siward and his Son,
Macduff, Menteith, Caithness,
Angus, Lennox, Ross, and Soldiers,
marching.*

Malcolm: Cousins, I hope the days are near at hand
    That chambers will be safe.
Menteith: We doubt it nothing.
Siward: What wood is this before us?
Menteith: The wood of Birnam.   5
Malcolm: Let every soldier hew him down a bough,
    And bear't before him; thereby shall we shadow
    The numbers of our host, and make discovery
    Err in report of us.
Soldier: It shall be done.   10
Siward: We learn no other but the confident tyrant
    Keeps still in Dunsinane, and will endure
    Our setting down before't.
Malcolm: 'Tis his main hope;
    For where there is advantage to be gone   15
    Both more and less have given him the revolt,
    And none serve with him but constrained things,
    Whose hearts are absent too.
Macduff: Let our just censures
    Attend the true event, and put we on   20
    Industrious soldiership.
Siward: The time approaches,
    That will with due decision make us know
    What we shall say we have and what we owe.
    Thoughts speculative their unsure hopes relate,   25
    But certain issue strokes must arbitrate:
    Towards which advance the war.

                     [Exeunt, marching]

4   *ague:* fever

5   *forced:* reinforced

6   *dareful:* defiantly; *beard to beard:* face to face

11   *my senses would have cool'd:* frozen (as in blood running cold)

12-14   *fell of hair . . . life were in't:* a horror story would make my hair stand on end

14   *I have supp'd full with horrors:* I have had my fill of horror.

15   *Direness:* horror

16   *Cannot once start:* can no longer startle

19   *She should have died hereafter:* Her death should have been later, at a time when it would have been possible to mourn her. Perhaps he means she should have waited for his death. Another possible meaning is that she would have died at some time, as we all have to die.

21-22   *To-morrow and to-morrow . . . day to day:* The future looks monotonous, slow-moving, hopeless.

23   *To the last syllable of recorded time:* to the end of human time

24-25   *all our yesterdays . . . dusty death:* All that the past has done is to lead ordinary, foolish people to their graves. ("Dusty death" refers to the line from the burial service: "For dust thou art and unto dust shalt thou return.")

25   *Out, out, brief candle:* Macbeth compares life to a candle

26   *Life's but a walking shadow:* insubstantial

26-28   *poor player . . . no more:* Life is an actor who performs only briefly, before his career is over.

28-30   *it is a tale . . . signifying nothing:* Life is a noisy story, but it is told by an insane person and has no meaning.

Scene 5

Dunsinane. Within the Castle.

*Enter, with drums and colours,
Macbeth, Seyton, and Soldiers.*

Macbeth: Hang out our banners on the outward walls;
   The cry is still, "They come": our castle's strength
   Will laugh a siege to scorn: here let them lie
   Till famine and the ague eat them up:
   Were they not forced with those that should be ours,   5
   We might have met them dareful, beard to beard,
   And beat them backward home.
                        [A cry within, of women]
                    What is that noise?
Seyton: It is the cry of women, my good lord.
                           [Exit]
Macbeth: I have almost forgot the taste of fears: 10
   The time has been, my senses would have cool'd
   To hear a night-shriek, and my fell of hair
   Would at a dismal treatise rouse, and stir
   As life were in't: I have supp'd full with horrors:
   Direness, familiar to my slaughterous thoughts,   15
   Cannot once start me.   *[Re-enter Seyton]*
                Wherefore was that cry?
Seyton: The queen, my lord, is dead.
Macbeth: She should have died hereafter;
   There would have been a time for such a word.   20
   To-morrow, and to-morrow, and to-morrow,
   Creeps in this petty pace from day to day,
   To the last syllable of recorded time;
   And all our yesterdays have lighted fools
   The way to dusty death. Out, out, brief candle!   25
   Life's but a walking shadow, a poor player
   That struts and frets his hour upon the stage
   And then is heard no more: it is a tale

36   *my watch:* my guard duty

45   *cling:* shrivels; *sooth:* true

46   *as much:* the same

47   *I pull in resolution:* I hold my confidence back. The metaphor suggests that the "horse" of Macbeth's confidence has been given free rein, but now he fears this was a mistake and that he has been betrayed.

48   *the fiend:* the witches

51   *Arm, arm, and out:* the news causes a change of plans

52   *avouches:* claims

53   *There is nor flying hence nor tarrying here:* One can neither escape nor stay.

54   *'gin:* begin; *the sun:* light, hence life

55   *wish the estate o' the world were now undone:* I wish the whole of creation were destroyed.

56   *wrack:* ruin

57   *harness:* armour

Told by an idiot, full of sound and fury,
Signifying nothing.   30
[*Enter a Messenger*]
Thou comest to use thy tongue; thy story quickly.
Messenger: Gracious my Lord,
    I should report that which I say I saw,
    But know not how to do it.
Macbeth: Well, say, sir.   35
Messenger: As I did stand my watch upon the hill,
    I look'd toward Birnam, and, anon, methought
    The wood began to move.
Macbeth: Liar, and slave!   [*Striking him*]
Messenger: Let me endure your wrath if't be not so;   40
    Within this three mile may you see it coming;
    I say, a moving grove.
Macbeth: If thou speak'st false,
    Upon the next tree shalt thou hang alive,
    Till famine cling thee: if thy speech be sooth,   45
    I care not if thou dost for me as much.
    I pull in resolution, and begin
    To doubt the equivocation of the fiend
    That lies like truth: "Fear not, till Birnam wood
    Do come to Dunsinane"; and now a wood   50
    Comes toward Dunsinane. Arm, arm, and out!
    If this which he avouches does appear,
    There is nor flying hence nor tarrying here.
    I'gin to be a-weary of the sun,
    And wish the estate o'the world were now undone.   55
    Ring the alarum-bell! Blow wind! come wrack!
    At least we'll die with harness on our back.
                                              [*Exeunt*]

2   *And show like those you are:* reveal yourselves; *worthy uncle:* Old Siward

4   *battle:* division; *we:* Malcolm is now using the royal plural

6   *order:* battle plan

8   *power:* army

Scene 6

*Dunsinane. A plain before the
Castle.*

*Enter, with drums and colours,
Malcolm, old Siward, Macduff,
and their army, with boughs.*

Malcolm: Now near enough; your leafy screens throw down,
And show like those you are. You, worthy uncle,
Shall, with my cousin, your right noble son,
Lead our first battle: worthy Macduff and we
Shall take upon us what else remains to do,   5
According to our order.
Siward: Fare you well.
Do we but find the tyrant's power to-night,
Let us be beaten, if we cannot fight.
Macduff: Make all our trumpets speak; give them all breath,   10
Those clamorous harbingers of blood and death.
                        [*Exeunt. Alarums continued*]

Act 5, Scenes 4, 5, and 6: Activities

1. Discuss with your group the effects Shakespeare achieves by alternating scenes between Macbeth and Malcolm's army. How might these scenes be directed in a film version? What would the audience gain or lose in the transfer from stage to film?

2. With a partner, rehearse and present to your group a reading of Macbeth's lines 10–30 in Scene 5. Discuss which reading is the most effective.

3. Imagine that Macbeth, too, has a sleep-walking scene. Working with a partner, write the script.

4. Hold an informal debate on the following topic: Macbeth's reaction to his wife's death shows that his love for her has dwindled to indifference.

5. Imagine that you are a radio reporter whose station has just asked for an up-date on events at Dunsinane. Plan and write a two-minute broadcast, then make the tape your listeners will hear. Compare your broadcast with others in the class.

6. Your last task as Lady Macbeth's lady-in-waiting is to make a statement to the press about the circumstances of and reasons for the queen's death. Either write or tape your comments.

For the next scenes . . .

Is revenge ever justified? In your personal journal, recall an incident in which you decided either to take revenge or that revenge would not be justified.

Act 5, Scenes 7 and 8

In these scenes . . .

On the battlefield, Macbeth feels trapped. At the same time, however, he clings to the third prophecy that he cannot be killed by anyone born of woman. His easy victory over Young Siward seems to increase his confidence. In the meantime, Macduff is looking for him, compelled to seek revenge. Siward announces the castle's surrender and, predicting victory, invites Malcolm to enter his rightful palace.

At last Macbeth and Macduff confront each other. Macbeth is reluctant to fight, feeling guilty enough for his slaughter of Macduff's family. He is still convinced that he cannot be killed, but Macduff's explanation that he was delivered by caesarian section and thus, technically, not born, forces upon Macbeth the full realization of the witches' deception or equivocation. Nevertheless, he refuses to yield; this time he will fight to the death.

1-2   *They have tied me . . . the course:* Macbeth's metaphor is from bear-baiting, a popular Elizabethan spectator sport. The bear was tied to a stake and attacked by dogs. The "course" was a round of the match.

22-23   *wretched kerns . . . staves:* the hired, miserable soldiers (mercenaries) who are paid to fight (*staves:* spears)

25   *undeeded:* unused

Scene 7

Another part of the Plain.

Enter Macbeth.

Macbeth: They have tied me to a stake; I cannot fly,
But bear-like I must fight the course. What's he
That was not born of woman? Such a one
Am I to fear, or none.
[*Enter young Siward*]
Young Siward: What is thy name?   5
Macbeth: Thou'lt be afraid to hear it.
Young Siward: No; though thou call'st thyself a hotter name
Than any is in hell.
Macbeth: My name's Macbeth.
Young Siward: The devil himself could not pronounce a   10
title
More hateful to mine ear.
Macbeth: No, nor more fearful.
Young Siward: Thou liest, abhorred tyrant; with my sword
I'll prove the lie thou speak'st.   15
                         [*They fight, and young Siward is slain*]
Macbeth: Thou wast born of woman.
But swords I smile at, weapons laugh to scorn,
Brandish'd by man that's of a woman born.   [*Exit*]
[*Alarums. Enter Macduff*]
Macduff: That way the noise is. Tyrant, show thy face!
If thou be'st slain and with no stroke of mine,   20
My wife and children's ghosts will haunt me still.
I cannot strike at wretched kerns, whose arms
Are hired to bear their staves; either thou, Macbeth,
Or else my sword, with an unbatter'd edge,
I sheathe again undeeded. There thou shouldst be;   25

26   *clatter:* noise and confusion; *greatest note:* great importance

27   *bruited:* announced

29   *gently render'd:* surrendered without resistance

30   *on both sides do fight:* Some of his men have changed sides; or they are not fighting seriously against us.

32   *professes:* declares

35   *That strike beside us:* who have joined our ranks; or who strike to deliberately miss us

By this great clatter, one of greatest note
Seems bruited: let me find him, fortune!
And more I beg not.   [*Exit. Alarums*]
[*Enter Malcolm and old Siward*]
Siward: This way, my lord; the castle's gently render'd:
The tyrant's people on both sides do fight;   30
The noble thanes do bravely in the war;
The day almost itself professes yours,
And little is to do.
Malcolm: We have met with foes
That strike beside us.   35
Siward: Enter, sir, the castle.
                    [*Exeunt. Alarum*]

1   *play the Roman fool:* suicide, by running on one's sword, was the honourable behaviour for defeated Roman generals.

2   *whiles I see lives:* while I see living enemies

10   *Than terms can give thee out:* than words can express

12   *intrenchant:* which cannot be wounded

13   *impress:* make an impression on

14   *vulnerable crests:* heads that can be wounded

15   *which must not:* is destined not to

18   *angel:* demon

19-20   *from his mother's womb/ Untimely ripp'd:* delivered prematurely, probably by Caesarian section.

22   *cow'd:* made fearful, intimidated; *better part of man:* his courage or, perhaps, his soul.

23   *juggling:* deceiving, cheating

24   *palter:* play, trifle, equivocate

28   *the show and gaze o' the time:* a sight for people to stare at

29-30   *We'll have thee . . . pole:* like a side-show marvel in a fair, his picture painted on a cloth and set up in front of a booth

Scene 8

Another part of the field.

Enter Macbeth.

Macbeth: Why should I play the Roman fool, and die
  On mine own sword? whiles I see lives, the gashes
  Do better upon them.
  [*Re-enter Macduff*]
Macduff: Turn, hell-hound, turn!
Macbeth: Of all men else I have avoided thee: 5
  But get thee back; my soul is too much charged
  With blood of thine already.
Macduff: I have no words:
  My voice is in my sword, thou bloodier villain
  Than terms can give thee out!   [*They fight*]   10
Macbeth: Thou losest labour:
  As easy mayst thou the intrenchant air
  With thy keen sword impress as make me bleed:
  Let fall thy blade on vulnerable crests;
  I bear a charmed life, which must not yield   15
  To one of woman born.
Macduff: Despair thy charm.
  And let the angel whom thou still hast served
  Tell thee, Macduff was from his mother's womb
  Untimely ripp'd.   20
Macbeth: Accursed be that tongue that tells me so,
  For it hath cow'd my better part of man!
  And be these juggling fiends no more believed,
  That palter with us in a double sense;
  That keep the word of promise to our ear,   25
  And break it to our hope. I'll not fight with thee.
Macduff: Then yield thee coward,
  And live to be the show and gaze o' the time:
  We'll have thee, as our rarer monsters are,

34   *baited:* tormented; *rabble:* common people

36   *opposed:* my opponent

37   *Yet I will try the last:* take the final test

Painted upon a pole, and underwrit, 30
'Here may you see the tyrant.'
Macbeth: I will not yield
To kiss the ground before young Malcolm's feet,
And to be baited with the rabble's curse.
Though Birnam wood be come to Dunsinane, 35
And thou oppos'd, being of no woman born,
Yet I will try the last. Before my body
I throw my warlike shield. Lay on, Macduff;
And damn'd be him that first cries 'Hold, enough!'
                    [*Exeunt, fighting. Alarums*]
[*Re-enter fighting, and Macbeth slain*]

Act 5, Scenes 7 and 8: Activities

1. Discuss with your group whether Macbeth's commitment to the final prophecy is more to his advantage or disadvantage. What other course of action might he have followed?

2. Write a description of your final feelings about Macbeth.

3. With a partner, look back to Act 1, Scene 2 and note the contrasts or ironic parallels with Act 5, Scenes 7 and 8. Write a summary of the changes in Macbeth.

4. a) If you had three choices – to commit suicide, to be taken prisoner, or to die fighting – which would you choose? Why? How do you feel about Macbeth's choice?

   b) If you felt compelled to obtain revenge, would taking your enemy prisoner or killing him give you greater satisfaction? Why? How do you feel about Macduff's choice? Share ideas with your group.

5. In your director's log
   a) Describe how you would direct the actor playing Macbeth to speak his lines in this scene. How should Macbeth appear to the audience?

   b) Describe how you think Macbeth should be killed and what effect you would like to achieve. What staging difficulties might you encounter? Would you choose to have him killed on stage or off stage?

For the next scene . . .

If your country had experienced great turmoil, how would you, as its leader, begin restoration?

Act 5, Scene 9

In this scene . . .

Now in possession of Dunsinane, Malcolm and Siward
are informed by Ross of the courageous death of
Young Siward. Macduff enters with Macbeth's head,
proclaims their victory, and declares Malcolm king.
The new king promises rewards and restoration of order, and asks for God's help and blessing. The moral
law is restored.

Stage direction—*Retreat:* the trumpet call to signal the end
of the fighting; *Flourish:* the trumpet call of triumph

2   *Some must go off:* die; *by these I see:* judging by the numbers
here

7   *prowess:* bravery

8   *In the unshrinking station:* the place from which he did not retreat

14   *before:* on the front of his body

17   *Had I as many sons as I have hairs:* a pun on hairs and heirs

19   *his knell is knoll'd:* The bell is rung to mark his death. Siward
implies that nothing more can be said.

23   *parted well and paid his score:* departed, died. He lived and
died as he should have.

25   *where stands:* probably carried on a pole

26   *the time is free:* Freedom has returned; order is restored.

27   *compass'd:* surrounded; *thy kingdom's pearl:* the great nobles
of Scotland, seen as the pearls surrounding a crown

Scene 9

Retreat. Flourish.

*Enter, with drum and colours,
Malcolm, old Siward, Ross, the
other Thanes, and Soldiers.*

Malcolm: I would the friends we miss were safe arrived.
Siward: Some must go off; and yet, by these I see,
   So great a day as this is cheaply bought.
Malcolm: Macduff is missing, and your noble son.
Ross: Your son, my lord, has paid a soldier's debt: 5
   He only lived but till he was a man;
   The which no sooner had his prowess confirm'd,
   In the unshrinking station where he fought,
   But like a man he died.
Siward: Then he is dead?   10
Ross: Ay, and brought off the field: your cause of sorrow
   Must not be measured by his worth, for then
   It hath no end.
Siward: Had he his hurts before?
Ross: Ay, on the front.   15
Siward: Why, then, God's soldier be he!
   Had I as many sons as I have hairs,
   I would not wish them to a fairer death:
   And so his knell is knoll'd.
Malcolm: He's worth more sorrow,   20
   And that I'll spend for him.
Siward: He's worth no more;
   They say, he parted well, and paid his score:
   And so, God be with him! Here comes newer comfort.
   [*Re-enter Macduff, with Macbeth's head*]
Macduff: Hail, king! for so thou art: behold, where stands   25
   The usurper's cursed head: the time is free:
   I see thee compass'd with thy kingdom's pearl,
   That speak my salutation in their minds;

32-34   *We shall not . . . even with you:* Using a business or banking metaphor, Malcolm assures his thanes that they will each be suitably repaid.

37   *be planted newly with the time:* be given a new beginning in a new age

39   *snares:* traps

40   *ministers:* agents

42-43   *by self . . . hands/ Took off her life:* killed herself

43-44   *and what needful . . . upon us:* other necessary things that demand our attention

45   *measure, time, and place:* with due order in every aspect

Whose voices I desire aloud with mine:
Hail, king of Scotland!   30
All: Hail, king of Scotland!   [*Flourish*]
Malcolm: We shall not spend a large expense of time
  Before we reckon with your several loves,
  And make us even with you. My thanes and kinsmen,
  Henceforth be earls, the first that ever Scotland   35
  In such an honour named. What's more to do,
  Which would be planted newly with the time,
  As calling home our exiled friends abroad
  That fled the snares of watchful tyranny,
  Producing forth the cruel ministers   40
  Of this dead butcher, and his fiend-like queen,
  Who, as 'tis thought, by self and violent hands
  Took off her life; this, and what needful else
  That calls upon us, by the grace of Grace,
  We will perform in measure, time, and place: 45
  So thanks to all at once and to each one,
  Whom we invite to see us crown'd at Scone.
                                        [*Flourish. Exeunt*]

Act 5, Scene 9: Activities

1. How do you feel about dying for your country? How would your parents feel if you were killed in battle? What do you think of Siward's reaction to his son's death? Make a journal entry or discuss with your group.

2. Ask one member of your group to play Malcolm and present a dramatic reading of his final speech (lines 32–47). Then hold a press conference, with other members of the group playing reporters. As is usual at press conferences, the media representatives may ask him personal questions, how he feels about past events, and what he plans for the future.

3. As directors, consider in a group:
   a) Would you show Macbeth's severed head? If so, how?

   b) What music would you choose for this scene, if any?

   c) Would you emphasize the defeat of evil or the restoration of good? How?

4. Describe or sketch the photograph that could appear on the front page of tomorrow morning's national Scottish newspaper. Include its caption. Then write the headline and opening paragraph for the accompanying news story.

5. Create a cartoon related in some way to Malcolm's success that would be suitable for publication in a newspaper or a news magazine.

6. Imagine that the witches are hovering around Dunsinane. With a partner, create a few lines of rhymed verse that express how they are reacting to the recent events.

7. Write a letter from Malcolm to Edward the Confessor, King of England, telling him of your victory and outlining your hopes for Scotland's future.

8. With a partner, role-play the conversation that the Old Man of Act 2, Scene 4 would now have with Ross.

Consider the Whole Play

1. With a partner, examine one of the following topics. Locate and make notes on appropriate examples throughout the play. Write your own observations in a short paper to share with others.

   a) Kingship (Remember to consider all four kings: Duncan, Edward the Confessor, Macbeth, Malcolm).

   b) Ambition (You could begin by listing on one side of a page all the positive features of Macbeth's ambition; then list on the other side all the negative features. You may wish to include Lady Macbeth in your discussion).

   c) Guilt (You could concentrate on either Macbeth or Lady Macbeth, or you could discuss both).

   d) Order (You could consider how nature appears to react to unnatural deeds, the gradual disintegration of political and personal relationships and how order is restored).

   e) Deceptive Appearances (You could begin to record these references using Act 1, Consider the Whole Act, activity 6, page 63).

   f) Fathers and Sons (You might consider not only the play's four father–son relationships, but the significance of the fact that Macbeth has no son).

   g) Sleep

   h) Loyalty and Patriotism

2. Many literary works have been inspired by *Macbeth*. Read one or more of these and write a report for presentation to the class. You might include an explanation

of how your work has used the original, the main ways in which it differs from the original, and a statement of how it increases and changes your understanding of the original.

Novels
Ray Bradbury, *Something Wicked This Way Comes* (Bantam, 1963). Although this novel makes no direct reference to the play (apart from the title), it describes two young boys' introduction to evil.

Agatha Christie, *By the Pricking of My Thumbs* (Fontana Collins, 1968). A fairly standard murder mystery story, in which the detective reacts to "the pricking of her thumbs" to solve the mystery.

Ngaio Marsh, *Light Thickens* (Fontana Collins, 1982). A murder mystery, set during a production of *Macbeth*. It also provides some insights into the play and to the "curse" of the play.

Short Story
John Updike, "Tomorrow and Tomorrow and So Forth", in Updike's *The Same Door and Other Stories* (Alfred A. Knopf, 1955). Reprinted in *The Secret Sharers and Other Great Stories* (Mentor, 1969). The story about a class studying *Macbeth* shows how the teacher is "brought down" by a student.

Drama
Tom Stoppard, "Cahoot's Macbeth" in *Dogg's Hamlet, Cahoot's Macbeth* (Faber and Faber, 1980). This short, satirical play is set in modern Czechoslovakia.

Poetry
Robert Frost, "Out, Out—" in *Complete Poems of Robert Frost* (Holt, Rinehart and Winston, 1947). This poem is about the sudden and tragic death of a teenage boy.

3. Choose one of the following activities:
   a) Write your own "ShrinkLit" in which you summarize the story of *Macbeth*, preferably in 10 to 20 lines of rhyme. Be as amusing and irreverent as you can.

If you wish to read some examples first, see *Shrinklits: Seventy of the world's towering classics cut down to size* by Maurice Sagoff (Workman, 1980).

b) Re-tell the major events of the play by writing a series of about 10 sensational headlines, the kind that would appear in a tabloid. Try to include some puns. Include other members of your group in this project. Once you begin writing, one headline will inspire another.

c) Rewrite *Macbeth* as a children's story. You will probably want to place less emphasis on the blood and horror and more emphasis on the supernatural and fantastic elements of the plot.

4. Work with the rest of your class on the edition of the *Dunsinane Times* that appears the day after Malcolm is proclaimed king. Your paper should have all the usual news and feature columns, including lead story, local, national, and international news, editorials, letters to the editor, weather, sports, business news, births, marriages, deaths and obituaries.

You might also include features such as science, travel, fashion, recipes and homemaking hints, gossip column, horoscopes, comics, the personal and classified columns, including situations vacant.

Find suitable illustrations, create collages, and provide sketches.

5. Choose one of the following activities:

a) Using one scene from the play, re-create it as a modern comic strip, in modern English and modern dress.

b) Design and sketch or paint a flier, the program cover, or the advertising poster that would be used for a production of the play. Choose a suitable location for this production (theatre, auditorium, park, old mansion, for example) and include information about it in your design.

c) Imagine that you have been commissioned to choreograph a five-minute ballet or mime that summarizes
the play. It is to be presented as a prologue and will
precede either a performance of the play or Verdi's
opera *Macbeth*. Choose the appropriate scene or
events. Describe the main movements and their purpose, and select and tape the music for your program. Perhaps a dancer in your class could perform
your ballet, or you could present it in mime.

d) Create a collage that captures the dominant mood
of either one scene or of the whole play.

e) Listen to a recording of a musical composition
inspired by the play. Among the best known are
the opera *Macbeth* by Guiseppe Verdi (1847),
Richard Strauss' *Macbeth* Symphonic Poem, opus
23 (1887–8, revised 1889–90), and Sir William Wal-
ton's *Macbeth* Theatre Incidental Music (1941).
Choose a section of the composition that you feel
best illustrates the composer's theme(s), play it to your
audience, and explain how it relates to the play or
has changed your understanding of some aspects of
the play.

6. Macbeth's attendant, Seyton, is now unemployed. As
armour-bearer is the only occupation he knows, he is
obliged to apply to Malcolm for a job. Write his resume,
giving the following information:

Name	Training and experience
Address	Special skills
Date of birth	Other relevant information
Marital status	Salary expected
Education	References
Position applied for	

You may prefer to write an application from the court
doctor, Lady Macbeth's lady-in-waiting, or the three
witches.

7. In the style of the witches, make some prophecies concerning the reign of Malcolm. You could take into account some of the Scottish history you or your classmates may have researched in activity #9, page 64.

8. Imagine you are directing a modern version of *Macbeth*. How will you present the witches? Will your ideas be more effective as a film or on stage?

   Prepare a speech you will make to your cast on the first day of rehearsals, explaining to them how your ideas and objectives for the production are based on your conception of the witches.

   Present your speech to your group or class.

9. Ask one member of your class to play a well-known feminist and another to play Lady Macbeth. The feminist should interview Lady Macbeth or hold an informal conversation with her.

   With your group, you could assist the feminist to prepare appropriate questions for her guest. They might include topics such as attitudes to women's education, professions, equal pay, rights, marriage, or children and parenting.

   Lady Macbeth should be given the topics ahead, so that she can prepare her responses.

10. Assume that the Macbeths survived. As a class project, conduct their trial. The roles to be played are the following: Macbeth and Lady Macbeth, their defence lawyer, the lawyer for the prosecution, a twelve member jury, a judge, and the Clerk of the Court. In addition, both lawyers may call a number of witnesses. Keep in mind the following:
    • The Clerk of the Court makes all announcements.
    • The judge presents the facts and determines the sentence. He also sustains or overrules objections from the lawyers.

- The jury acts on the facts. Any member of the jury may ask for clarification during the trial.
- The accused is presumed innocent until proven guilty.
- The prosecution must establish guilt beyond a reasonable doubt.
- Persons who assist or counsel in the commission of a crime can also be found guilty.

11. With your group, describe and explain the effects of some of the dramatic devices you notice in a favourite television show. They may include devices such as repeated use of images and symbols and/or key words or phrases. What setting, music and other sound effects, camera techniques, and lighting are used?

   Share your observations about some of the dramatic devices used by Shakespeare in *Macbeth*. They might include your observations about the varied settings in time and place, irony, suspense, contrasts, repeated references to blood, and images of clothing, animals, health, disease, and feasting.

   Choose one of the above dramatic devices and, by preparing a shooting script or by making notes in your director's log, explain how you would film or stage an example of its use. The success of your project could be assessed by the success the rest of the class has in grasping the effect you are trying to achieve.

12. Research and present to your class a report on "The Curse of Macbeth." Explain why actors call the play "The Scottish Play" or "The Unmentionable," and why Macbeth is "The Thane" and his wife is "The Lady." You might include a description of how an actor makes amends for breaking the "rules" about staging the play. Include some examples of the "curse" at work.

13. If you are interested in Shakespeare's main source for *Macbeth* locate a copy of Raphael Holinshed's *Chronicles of England, Scotland, and Ireland* (1577) or use the

relevant excerpts that are reprinted in many editions of *Macbeth*.

Note where Shakespeare altered, added, omitted, or in other ways changed Holinshed's account.

Consider why Shakespeare may have made these changes and what their effects are.

Present your report to the class.

14. In Act 2, Scene 3, the porter makes several references to events that would have been familiar to Shakespeare's audience. One of them is to an equivocator who was, in fact, Father Garnet, a Jesuit who, at his trial, defended his right to equivocate.

    With the help of your librarian, research the Gunpowder Plot (1605) and Garnet's involvement. Consider how this research contributes to your understanding of the play.

    Present your report to the class.

15. With a partner, research and present a report on two or three contemporary figures who gained sudden political or social prominence but did not prepare realistically for their new lives. You could compare the contemporary figures with the Macbeths and include the similarities and differences between them in your presentation.

16. Research and present a report on one of the following:
    • The Elizabethans' belief about an ordered universe that was revealed in religion, politics, and science.
    • The belief of James I and his Stuart descendants in the Divine Right of Kings. You could in your report use some quotations from *Macbeth* that illustrate this concept.